Islington

The First

2000

Years

www.pamela-shields.co.uk

www.scribbling4bread.wordpress.com

Front cover: The Kings Head's Theatre, Upper Street

Back Cover: Duncan Terrace

Front and Back cover design: Mark Playle

www.playlephotography.co.uk

About the author

Pamela Shields has earned a crust as an art teacher, press officer and journalist. She was born in Epsom Surrey, grew up in Wales and lived in London for 20 years, ten of which were in Islington where she was a tourist guide and tutored the Guiding for Tourists Course at City University. She left the seductive distractions of Islington to concentrate on writing and went on to publish *Essential Islington From Boadicea to Blair; Hertfordshire A-Z, The Private Lives of Hertfordshire Writers, Hertfordshire Secrets & Spies, The Little Book of Hitchin and Royal Hertfordshire Murders & Misdemeanours.*

The rights of Pamela Shields to be identified as the Author of this work has been asserted in accordance with the Copyright, Designs and Patents Act 1988.

All rights reserved. No part of this book may be reprinted or reproduced or utilised in any form or by any electronic, mechanical or other means, now known or hereafter invented, including photocopying and recording, or in any information storage or retrieval system, without the permission in writing from the Publishers.

First Published by HHH Publishing 2000

Second Edition by Shoestring Publications 2010

Islington has been here forever. The bones of a straight tusked elephant and an axe dated 20,000BC were found in King's Cross Road. Since then, twenty more axes (one at Highbury New Park) have turned up. In 1812 during the excavation for The Regent's Canal the vertebra of a crocodile was found under the cellars of built up Pentonville.

In the beginning was...the water. Today we have many reasons for choosing where we live, once, there was only one, access to clean drinking water. Islington had plenty, its name, like that of Keats is 'writ in water' (unique in London it still has an excess of ground water). It lies in the Thames basin, where sand, gravel and limestone provide a superb filter. Water settles between the grains and (before Mr Macadam invented tar) wherever it met London clay it burst through to form a spring. Blessed with three rivers, Islington must once have looked like Venice.

Wheat, rye, barley and oats thrive; fields are full of hay; milk is so abundant it never needs to be watered to save money; pigs forage in the forests and ox graze in the pastures. Soon, the reason for Islington's existence is to serve the City of London, a ready market. This is city dwellers nearest place for hawking, hunting and archery especially when the Moor Gate was hacked out of the old Roman wall. This was the city's back garden. Its nearest cultivated fields provided it with dairy products and hay until the 1800s.

But geology alone can't explain Islington's enduring popularity. Market towns all over the UK were equally blessed by nature. For some inexplicable reason, non-conformists to the downright rebellious, by accident or design, seem to have been drawn here at some time of their lives and Islington's astonishing story belongs to them.

450 BC

Celts arrive. They speak brythonic (welsh) the oldest language in Europe (where we get Briton from). Islington is a hilly part of the Great Forest of Middlesex. Evidence survives in street names: Back Street Hill, Eyre Street Hill, Herbal Hill, Hermes Hill, Highbury Hill, Highgate Hill, Rising Hill, Saffron Hill and Vine Hill. Where there are hills there are wells, brooks, streams and rivers. Celts call this place Yseldon; welsh for 'the place of wells'. Of the eighteen identified, many have names: Bagnigge (probably the name of the landowner), Chiswell (ceosel is Saxon for flint/pebble) Fagge, Goswell (possibly God's Well) Loder's, Rede, Rad, Skinner, Tod, the famous Clerken Well and Sadler's Wells. The wells ran into the river Wall Brook (Walbrooke) Haca's Ey (Hackney) Brook and 'The River of Wells'. The Walbrooke started at the Angel and ran down into the City. The poor built shanties along its banks and the rich their houses. The lane running alongside became a road; the road became a highway, then a high street. By 1600, the river was forgotten. The Walbrook is now City Road. Hackney Brook ('Haca' was a Danish landowner, 'Ey' is Danish for 'island') ran west/east from Isledon Road, Gillespie Road, Riversdale Road, Clissold Park on to Abney Park and the river Lea The River of Wells started at Hampstead (it still does), ran through King's Cross, Farringdon Road, Holborn and on to what was once known as The Tames (welsh for 'dark river').

61 AD

Battle Bridge. The battle was possibly Celts v. Romans. Boadicea (Queen of the Iceni tribe in East Anglia) v. General Suetonius. She committed suicide rather than surrender. Battle Bridge crossed The River of Wells at what is now King's Cross station. Academics rubbish the legend but have no better idea where the battle took place. In 1937 Islington Council re-named Buckingham Street Boadicea Street.

200

The Romans have finished their defensive wall around Londinium. They use the ten acre smooth field (Smithfield) outside the north west perimeter as a horse market and as a crematorium.

628

Honorius, Archbishop of Canterbury, divides England into parishes. Islington is the parish of St Mary. St Paul's Cathedral owns the freehold of the church, Our Lady of Islington (there's a statue of the Virgin outside) in Upper Street. Even today there is still a Prebendary Stall in St. Paul's. A prebendary is a canon or administrator, a prebend is a stipend. When attending services, Prebendaries sit in particular seats at the back of the choir stalls. Today Prebendaries have specific duties in relation to the election of bishops and preach in the Cathedral.

Celtic 'Yseldon' is now Saxon 'Isendone'. Isen was Saxon for iron (some wells are chalybeate with a high iron content). They call the 'river of wells', the 'Fleet' (fast flowing), the road north 'Hohl Weg' (Holey Way) and the smooth field 'smetha felde' (Smithfield). Hohl Weg (Holloway) is holey because of drovers and cattle on their way to Smithfield, the world's largest cattle market where the Romans bought and sold horses. The market puts Clerkenwell on the international map. Yseldon/Isendone/Islington Road, London's first bypass, starts at Smithfield, continues along St. John Street, Upper Street and Holloway Road. It's called The Great North Road. Because of the drovers and Smithfield Market, Islington Road is known all over Britain. Isendone is thriving, awash with brewers, farmers, saddlers, horse collar makers, coopers, blacksmiths, cobblers, weavers, bakers, glaziers, carpenters and tailors. This is the City's back garden and playground with an endless supply of dairy products and hay for horses. It takes a huge leap of imagination to picture thousands of animals lumbering along Upper Street but they did, for almost two thousand years. Drovers are a familiar sight until the mid 1800s when cattle arrive by rail to meet their maker. They are the equivalent of today's juggernauts and about as popular but extremely important in the growth of Islington. Drovers spend winter evenings knitting thick woollen socks and rub the insides with soap to prevent blisters. Before a drove, they wrap stiff brown paper made waterproof by soap around the socks and dry soap the inside of wooden clogs. Their fast food diet on the road includes a handful of oats washed down with water and a ram's horn of whisky to help kick start them on frosty mornings and to warm them before settling down at night among the herd which they dare not leave, on constant lookout for wolves and highwaymen. A thousand cattle a drove is normal so the noise (let alone the mounds of steaming dung left behind) is deafening with drovers shouting at the cattle, dogs barking rounding them up and the huge beasts making their dissatisfaction with their lot very vocal. Drovers are the postmen and news reporters of their day. Walking at two miles an hour they catch up with gossip along the way. Near London, cattle drovers are joined by sheep drovers from Lincolnshire, Suffolk and Norfolk (pigs, famously stubborn, refuse to be driven so are raised in Smithfield). Geese and turkeys have their feet dipped in warm tar, sawdust and crushed cockleshells before being wrapped in canvas 'shoes'. Turkeys try to roost in the trees overnight and hours of precious daylight are wasted next day getting them down. Although unpopular intruders into Islington's rural peace (as are the thousands of motorists who pour through today) drovers (unlike drivers) are respected. Known for their honesty, they're in trust to traders to deliver large sums of money to City businessmen and act as escorts to travellers and pilgrims. The job is stressful, so how they cheer when they get to High Gate and finally look down on the spire of St Paul's (the tallest in Europe) and the great City of London spread out beneath them. After three tortuous weeks on the road, it's downhill all the way from here and when they climb the unavoidable four hundred foot ascent to go home at least they're cattle free. Those who do well at market pay for 'lifts' home. Where Hollow Way meets Hornsey Road they cheer the highwayman hanging from the gibbet. The corpse is baked hard and covered in tar so lasts for months, years even. These contorted black figures swinging eerily in the moonlight are a constant reminder of the wages of sin meant to act as a deterrent but for many life is so awful death is a welcome release. Here, drovers tie a personal possession to the collar of a trained dog and send it on ahead to their favourite Islington inn to make sure of a bed. When they arrive they can relax because here a closed shop trades union is practised. Officials licensed by the City Corporation put the emaciated beasts out to their final pasture to be fattened up for sale. They look after the grazing herds before a second contingent leads the animals down Islington Road to Smithfield Bar. On the last leg, if suitably bribed by thieves and pickpockets, they stampede the cattle to cause chaos. This is where the saying 'a bull in a china shop' comes from. After the sale, a third set of drovers, paid for by butchers, take the cattle to slaughterhouses along the banks of the Fleet. Inns spring up all over Islington (twenty-three on Islington Road alone) and many put on entertainment. Bets are taken on bare knuckle boxing matches between farmers and drovers.

The First Millennium

1000

The Bishop of London starts what became known as The Smithfield Burnings. Criminals are hung, drawn and quartered, heretics are burnt. The smell of burning flesh is already familiar; the smooth field was once a Roman crematorium. The field is also used for archery, hawking and entertainment.

1016

Another battle at what would in the 1800s become King's Cross. Saxon v. Dane, Edmund v. Canute. Edmund wins and a well springs up which he dedicates to St Chad (Chad Street) a place of pilgrimage. It was covered over in the 1860s to make way for the railway.

1068

William the Conqueror wipes out the English aristocracy and gives their lands to the barons who fought for him. He gives south Islington to Jordan de Briset, north Islington to Ralph de Berners and Tottenham to Robert de Bruis (Bruis is near Cherbourg). Finsbury is 'Fiennes Borough' so central Islington may have gone to the Norman de Fiennes. William diverts some of Islington's streams into the City and builds a prison on the Fleet (Farringdon Road) which survives in one form or another for eight hundred years.

When he counts heads for the Domesday Book, there are twenty seven in Islington, forty-one in Newington and nine in Tollington (Hornsey).

1099

When the Crusaders take Jerusalem tourists want to visit the Holy City. Pilgrims from the north who pass through Islington on their way south walk with the drovers.

1100

St Marys' Nunnery, Clerkenwell is the first in London by a hundred years. When Baron de Briset gives fourteen acres near Clerkenwell Green for a Benedictine Nunnery dedicated to the Virgin, The Clerk's Well enters written history. *Ecclesia Sanctae Mariae de Fonte Clericorum*, The Church of Saint Mary by the Clerk's Well.

1113

A sort of Thomas Cook is set up in Jerusalem to cater for tourists. It calls itself The Sovereign Military Order of The Hospital of St John of Jerusalem or The Knights of the Order of the Hospital of St John the Baptist of Jerusalem. A bit of a mouthful, they're called The Knights of St John, the Knights Hospitallers or simply The Hospitallers. Knights wear long black nighties (with a gold embroidered cross) when they go to war and a white one during peace.

A separate, crack fighting unit, the Military Knights Hospitallers is later formed to protect pilgrims on their journey.

1123

Henry I gives his special servant Rahere a corner of Smithfield to build St. Bartholomew the Great, Britain's first public free hospital, to commemorate his drowned son William (named after Henry's father William the Conqueror) heir to the throne. He grants what will become known as 'Barts' a Royal Charter:

'I will maintain and defend this place even as my crown - and let this place be perpetually defended by the protection of Kings.'

St. Bartholomew's Fair, which puts Clerkenwell on the international map, is held every 24 August (St Bartholomew's Feast Day). The Worshipful Companies of Mercers and Merchant Tailors ensure 'fair trading'. Huge revenues are collected from Cloth Fair. The first bale from the loom is cut by the Lord Mayor to declare the fair open, a ceremony still carried on today all over the world every time anyone cuts a ribbon to open an event. The pub sign, Hand and Shears, Cloth Fair, commemorates the tradition. The pub doubles as a 'pieds poudres' (dusty feet) Court when the Fair is on. Instant summary justice is served in what was dubbed a Pie Powder Court held at all large fairs until as late as 1970.

1140

The Knights of St. John need an English HQ. Clerkenwell is the ideal location so the de Briset family give land 'for the maintenance of soldiers against the Turks and infidels'. Hospitallers paint stone crosses, some red, some white (as in Whitecross Street) to mark out their boundaries. The Prior of St John is the third most influential man in England, next in rank to the King and Archbishop of Canterbury. Not only is he Grand Prior of all England he is High Lord Treasurer, Chancellor of the Realm and First Baron. St John's is a self-contained community with ships on the Fleet, orchards, vineyards (e.g. Vineyard Walk - there's nothing new about English wine) counting house, dormitories, distillery, brewery, kitchens and fish ponds. There's an armoury, visitors parlours, schoolhouse, wood yards and a laundry. The church with its circular nave has three chapels, vestry and crypt (still there). Here live the prior, three chaplains, fifteen deacons, the keeper of the keys, the parish priest, paying guests and their servants, pharmacists, janitors, millers, slaughterers, brewers, pig keepers, attorneys, clerks and lots of horses. The Priory has everything except actual Knights who are on site Reps in the Holy Land or guiding the faithful there. Hospitality by the Knights is offered all the way from

Clerkenwell to Jerusalem and pilgrims will hear eight different languages (tongues) represented by the eight pointed cross along the way. The waiting list of lads wanting to be a Knight is long but getting accepted into the Order is not easy. An English Knight of St John must be of legitimate noble birth from four descents on both sides, be over twenty, a bachelor, free from debts, a free man and chaste. If assigned to the Military he'll wear a red nightie with a white cross if a Hospitaller, a black one (now known as the Maltese Cross). Islington Road is now also known as St John Street Road. Poor old Clerkenwell Green running down to the Fleet shrinks to a wedge shaped lump between the Knights (Jerusalem Passage) and the Nuns of St.Mary's (Clerkenwell Close).

1154

The nuns of St. Mary dedicate their church to St. James the Less, patron saint of pilgrims. It survives today in the shape of St James, Clerkenwell Close. The Three Kings pub is on the site of the sleeping quarters of the nun's servants.

1174

William FitzStephen, private secretary to Thomas Becket, writes the biography of his murdered boss. Becket was called Becket of London. Becket's London included St John Street, Turn Mill Street and the Clerken Well on the banks of the Fleet half a mile from St Paul's, a favourite watering hole for parish clerks ('clerken' was Anglo-Saxon plural for clerk). This is where they put on mystery and passion plays to teach the Bible to illiterates. The steep banks of the Fleet valley make a superb, natural amphitheatre.

1185

Bishop Heraclius of Jerusalem consecrates the priory church of the Knights of St. John. With him at the ceremony is Henry II. Asked by Heraclius to lead the next crusade, Henry refuses, offering a donation instead.

1190

The rich build houses in Turn Mill Street and their 'necessity houses' called 'bogs' over the Fleet. Richard of Devizes, monk and chronicler of London is shocked by: '...smooth skinned lads, Moors, pretty boys, effeminates, belly dancers, sorceresses, extortionates, night wanderers, magicians, beggars and buffoons' in Cow Cross Street around the corner.

1199

King John (reluctant signatory of Magna Carta) stays at St John's Priory for a month to prepare for his coronation.

1225

Henry III grants citizens the privilege to hunt within twenty miles of London once a year. They use an abandoned royal hunting lodge at the top of St. John Street. Why did royalty abandon it? Was there already nothing worth hunting in the area? It may be that pilgrims who arrive after the city gates are closed for the night use it for shelter and this may be the beginning of the Angel Inn.

People couldn't read so inn signs were visual aids. This one showed the Angel of the Annunciation with the Virgin Mary. Drovers tended to stay at the Old Red Lion opposite and the 'Wayte Lion' (White Lion Street) nearby. Three hundred years later, Henry VIII, in his anti Pope pogrom, destroyed all depictions of the Virgin Mary so the inn sign ended up showing only the angel.

1253

The de Berners of Berners Borough (Barnsbury) give 'Barts' a sizeable chunk of real estate. The 'canon's borough' (Canonbury) is bounded by Upper Stroet (street) Lower Ride (road) and Hopping Lane. Anglo-Saxon stroets had buildings on both sides; a 'ride' was uninhabited, meant for horse riders (traffic diversion) Lower Road (Essex Road) was/is literally lower than Upper Street. Hopping Lane (St. Paul's Road) cut through hop fields. It was so narrow that people had to hop out of the way of traffic (still do).

1254

Prince Edward (later Edward I) spends his honeymoon at St John's Priory with Eleanor of Castile, famous for all those Eleanor Crosses.

1271

Lady Alicia de Barowe, whose antecedents were in the Domesday Book gives the Lordship of the High Burh (Highbury) its manor house and three hundred wooded acres to The Knights of St John.

1282

Having killed the Prince of Wales, Edward I gives Wales his new born son (Edward II) who 'spoke no English'. The first son of every English monarch ever since is the Prince of Wales. Welsh barons arrive in London to pay homage to Edward I. Billeted in Islington they're furious when locals laugh at their clothes. Edward, needing archers for defence of the realm, establishes a Territorial Army (TA, nucleus of the Honourable Artillery Company (HAC) in City Road) out of these loyal Welsh volunteers, the world's finest bowmen. The so called 'English' longbow is Welsh. They invented it and the two finger insult (the bow was so powerful it took two fingers instead of one to draw). A Marcher Lord left a record of a battle in South Wales in which one of his men was hit by an arrow from a longbow which pierced his chain mail into his thigh, wooden saddle and horse's flank. The longbow was so efficient it lasted until the advent of the modern rifle. The longbow will win Crecy (1346) and Poitiers (1356) for Edward III.

1300

Saffron is used in cooking to disguise the taste and smell of rancid meat so thousands of crocuses are planted near Smithfield Market (Saffron Hill).

1309

Robert de Bruis, disgusted by the torture of William Wallace (plaque commemorating Wallace on the wall of 'Barts') leaves the English Court to claim the Scottish throne. His lands in England including Bruis/Bruce Castle in Tottenham revert to the Crown.

1348

The Black Death. With city streets piled high with rotting corpses, many survivors move to Islington. The graveyards are full so Sir Walter de Manny (soldier hero written up in Froissart) buys land from Barts to use as a plague pit (Charterhouse Square). Stowe in his 1598 Survey of London mentions a cross dated 1349 put up to commemorate 50,000 buried there but the population of London in 1348 was only 45,000 so that year couldn't have seen off more than 25,000 although in the end the plague killed between 60,000 and 100,000.

1350

Seven elm trees are planted in a circle with a walnut tree in the middle at Page Green Tottenham. In 1831 this will be Seven Sisters Road.

1361

Second wave of the plague, *pestis puerorum*, because it kills children. More citizens move to Islington.

1369

The Military Training Act is passed to guarantee trained bowmen for the costly, futile, Hundred Years War with France. Edward III has made the practising of archery compulsory. With no room within the city walls, the TA plays bows and arrows in Smithfield.

1371

Walter de Manny founds a monastery, a 'chartreuse' ('isolated country house') modelled on the one in Chartreuse, Switzerland where the thick sweet green liqueur comes from. Chartreuse has come down to us as Charterhouse although it has nothing to do with charters. He commissions Yvele the King's master mason (he invented English Perpendicular for the nave of Westminster Abbey and rebuilt parts of the Tower of London). When Sir Walter dies, he's buried at the foot of the high altar. Five hundred years later (1941) German bombs reveal his resting place.

This year, Sir Robert Hales, Prior of St John's, the hated tax gatherer (dubbed Hob the Robber) demolishes modest Highbury Manor and builds a magnificent moated castle. Hence the London Underground logo for Highbury & Islington station. The castle is to locals what Versailles will be to sans-culottes in revolutionary France.

1377

Around this time, Dick Whittington trudged up New North Road, Canonbury Road and Holloway Road heading north. Until 1999, all the Mayors of London led by the Mayor of Islington walked the walk every year, but the route was changed via St Paul's and the Tower because it's prettier! Dick wasn't going home, that was in Pauntley, Gloucester, in the west. Some sources say that when he arrived in London he went to St John's Priory and got a job. At the bottom of Highgate Hill, a daunting four hundred foot ascent, he stops for a rest and hears The Great Bell of Bow rung every night at nine o'clock to warn travellers that the City gates are about to close and to tell apprentices that they can stop work. Dick interprets the bell as an omen telling him if he goes back he will be Lord Mayor of London (he was elected Mayor in 1397, 1416 and 1419). Legend has it he showed people precisely where he turned back. In 1460, Richard Whittington, his great-nephew, built a mansion in Pauntley. In it was a statue of a boy with a cat (now in Gloucester museum). The Islington Coat of Arms incorporate those of Whittington.

1381

The Peasants Revolt. The Hundred Years War with France rumbles on. To pay for it, a tax of one groat (four pence) was levied. It didn't bring in nearly enough so a higher tax was imposed. When this too proved insufficient a poll tax of one shilling was forced on everyone over the age of fifteen regardless of income. Robert Hales and his sadist tax collectors inspect children's genitalia to assess their age resulting in contempt for the Hospitallers. The poor are furious to be sacrificed for the King's dream of ruling France. What did war between the ruling classes in a never seen foreign land mean to them? Why should they pay for it? Inevitable tax evasion leads to inevitable forced extraction. Even without The Poll Tax, the country is demoralised. England is losing to France, defeat is imminent and the hated war has caused rocketing inflation. Wages are pegged and peasants are treated worse than animals. Because of a serious shortage of labour following The Black Death plans are afoot to return free men back into slavery. They are forced to work on the squire's land for nothing and not allowed to leave the village without his permission. Wat Tyler camps on Clerkenwell Green before doing something no-one, not even William the Conqueror or Adolf Hitler, managed. He takes London. Wat sets fire to St. John's Priory. The fire burns for eight days and only the crypt survives. Jack Straw and his gang go to Highbury Castle and burn it down. The blaze is seen by rebels miles away in St. Albans on their way to join the march. The ruins are dubbed Jack Straw's Castle. Highbury Castle is never rebuilt, present day Leigh Road is the filled in moat. Wat goes to the Tower and chops off the heads of Prior Hales and Simon of Sudbury, Archbishop of Canterbury.

Saturday 15 June. The King's men line up outside Barts, Wat's men outside Smithfield Market. Richard II, his bodyguard Squire Standish and Mayor William Walworth meet Tyler who is alone in the middle of the Square. All are on horseback. Walworth, apprenticed as a lad to the Fishmonger's Company, owned many of the brothels burned down by the rioters and is a Founder of Charterhouse which he assumes (wrongly) Wat intends to burn down not realising that the only properties destroyed belong to Hospitallers. Wat can't resist the grand gesture. He nonchalantly bends down, scoops water from a puddle, rinses his mouth and with an expression of contempt spits it out at the feet of the King. A furious Walworth catches him off guard and stabs him; Standish draws his sword and finishes him off. Both are knighted on the spot. Leaderless and outnumbered Wat's men are escorted by Richard past St John's which is still burning, out to the moor fields where they disperse and go home. There is no commemoration of Wat Tyler in Smithfield. On the contrary, the City of London honours Walworth.

1382

Richard II and his Queen (Anne of Bohemia) celebrate their wedding with a pageant at Smithfield. The MC is Geoffrey (*The Canterbury Tales*) Chaucer.

1390

Richard II and Queen Anne are at the Clerken Well to watch a play about the creation. During the interval, four days later, cast and audience move on to Skinners Well (today's Skinner Street) to watch Part Two.

1397

Richard II makes Dick Whittington, Lord Mayor of London.

1399

The usurper, Henry IV, is at St. John's Priory preparing for his coronation (even though we already have a king, his cousin, Richard II).

1404

The Abbess of St. Mary's orders gates be erected facing Clerkenwell Green. Locals take them down in the night because she has encroached on their common land.

1405

Sir William Walworth lays the first stone of the first monk's cell at Charterhouse. The life of a Carthusian looks good. For six days he prays for the souls of the dead. Sundays are for socialising. The so called 'cells' are two storey four room cottages each with its own herb garden. The cottage wall abutting the cloister has a service hatch for delivery of meals on sandals. A servant (secular/lay brother/second class monk) responsible for the day to day running of the monastery places a meal in a hatch the cloister side and closes the door. The monk opens a door his side and takes his vittles. In this way he needn't pass the time of day. The garden wall has a service hatch too so that the 'night soil' collector can collect the monk's holy poo.

When a novice is given his white habit and cowl he's told it's also his shroud. When he dies he has no coffin and no memorial. He's laid, in his habit, face down in the earth in an unmarked grave. Today, a nameless, wooden cross marks the grave of a modern Carthusian.

1409

Theatre Review: 'Great play at Skynners Welle ... there were to see the same the most part of the nobles and gentles in England'...

1413

Henry V is at St. John's Priory preparing for his coronation. His childhood friend and staunch ally Sir John Oldcastle (Lord Cobham) who lives up the road (Clerkenwell Fire Station is on the site) has just escaped from the Tower where he was imprisoned for heresy. His followers in Clerkenwell hide him from the authorities for four years.

1415

(i) The Fiennes family give the moor fields to the Corporation of London. A gate is put into the city wall to give citizens direct access: 'Thomas Fawconer, Lord Mayor, caused the wall of the city to be broken toward the said moor and built the postern called Moor Gate for the ease of citizens to walk that way upon causeys towards Iseldon'.

(ii) Written records of The Old Red Lion, St John Street, begin.

1417

(i) Oldcastle's Rebellion. Sir John Oldcastle leader of the Lollards ('lollaert' - Dutch derogatory term for 'mumbler') denounces Christian transubstantiation (bread into body, wine into blood) all wars and capital punishment. The Good Lord Cobham is hanged in chains and burnt alive on Christmas Day as a heretic.

(ii) The Lord Mayor closes brothels within city walls. Turnmill Street, Clerkenwell, outside jurisdiction, enjoys extra business.

1420

The Priory of St. Bartholomew the Great is annexed from the hospital (Barts) for administrative purposes. Some sources say Barts has two thousand beds, other, two hundred.

1460

Sweet, gentle, Henry VI is brought as a prisoner to London. He is met in Islington by the Earl of Warwick, who arrested him in the name of King Edward IV. His golden spurs are removed from his feet. This is symbolic of public disgrace. He manacles Henry's legs to his stirrups and takes him to the Tower. Henry hasn't done anything wrong (except denounce war) but became unbalanced and went walkabout.

1473

William Pole, a rich merchant, contracts leprosy and opens a leper hospital where Whittington Hospital is today. A stone cross is put up on the roadside to warn passers by. They call it the Whittington Stone so his story is already legend.

1483

(i) Our Lady of Islington, Upper Street (St. Mary's, Islington's one and only C of E until 1820) is rebuilt. Ninety two feet long, twenty eight foot high, fifty-four foot wide it's made of stone, boulders, flint and pebbles with a tiled roof and turret. A statue of the Virgin is outside.

(ii) Locals enclose a spring in Highbury Fields (in front of 14 Highbury Place). The conduit survives four hundred years. As Highbury is owned by the Knights of St John Clerkenwell, the conduit becomes Crown property when Henry VIII disbands the Order.

1485

Richard III faces his critics at St John's Priory and lies. He says he has no intention of marrying his niece Elizabeth of York.

1487

Henry Tudor (Henry VII) is ceremoniously welcomed in Islington by the Lord Mayor. He has just returned from the north where he saw off the impostor Lambert Simnel.

1499

Thomas More, law student, takes lodgings in Charterhouse Square to be near the Carthusians. He stays four years and seriously considers joining the

Order. Lawyer or monk, he would have met the same fate. Henry VIII executed him and the Carthusians.

1504

One hundred and twenty-years after Wat Tyler burnt it down Prior Dowcra rebuilds St. John's Gate. It's still there.

1509

(i) Prior William Bolton of St Bartholomew's builds the Canonbury Tower complex.

(ii) Henry VIII knights his PA, William Compton, and gives him Bruce Castle. William's grandson, also William, through marriage, will own Canonbury Tower.

1517

Sir Richard Cloudesley leaves his 'stoney fields 'to the borough. By 1999 his bequest is earning £500k p.a for charities.

1520

Henry VIII takes Dowcra, Prior of St John's and Thomas More to meet the King of France on the Field of the Cloth of Gold (his tents were yellow).

1529

Lord Latimer intends to marry Catherine Parr so buys a house in Charterhouse Square near her brother, Sir William Parr 'because it stands in good air out of the press of the City'.

1530

The Statute of Highways is passed. Property owners in St John Street are ordered to 'mend their ways' (repair the road outside their front door).

1535

Clerkenwell is the centre of world attention when John Houghton, Prior of Charterhouse is executed for treason (refusing to recognise Henry VIII Head of the Supreme Church in England). Fellow Carthusians are 'boyled in oyle' at Smithfield. Charterhouse is now Crown property.

1536

Henry VIII gives newly built Canonbury Tower, the ruins of Highbury Castle and its three hundred acres to Thomas Cromwell. He allows Whittington Hospital to stay open but closes the chapel.

1537

Henry VIII grants Letters Patent (special privileges stamped with The Great Seal) to the Artillery Company.

1539

Henry VIII sells St Bartholomew the Great (except for the Quire which is kept for public worship) to Sir Richard Rich a particularly evil man. Public outcry saves Barts Hospital. He sells St Mary's Nunnery to Sir Edward North (locals are allowed to use the church). He closes all wells dedicated to saints and orders all statues of the Virgin (including the one outside St.Mary's Upper Street) be destroyed. Our Lady of Islington is now St.Mary's.

1540

Henry VIII closes St. John's Priory.

1541

After arranging Henry's disastrous marriage to Anne of Cleves, Thomas Cromwell loses Canonbury Tower, Highbury Castle and his head. His property reverts to the Crown. Henry gives church land near Clerkenwell Green (once owned by the nuns of St.Mary's) to Sir Thomas Chaloner, Privy Councillor, envoy to Spain, Scotland and France. He also gives him Guisborough Priory, Yorkshire, valuable for the mining of alum. Alum, used to fix dyes, was imported from the Papal States until Henry VIII was excommunicated so an industry was founded to process the shale which contained aluminium sulfate. Today alum is used as an aftershave and in styptic pencils to prevent bleeding from shaving cuts.

It's also used in depilatory waxes used for the removal of body hair, underarm deodorant and in fire extinguishers to smother chemical and oil fires.

1543

(i) Henry VIII incorporates The Artillery Company in City Road within the Guild of St. George.

(ii) Catherine Parr of Charterhouse Square, widow of Lord Latimer, marries Henry VIII. She will go down in history as his sixth and last wife.

(iii) The King's Head is built (or re-built) in Upper Street. Was the eponymous 'King' Henry VIII?

(iv) Margaret Fowler Savile, 19, daughter of Thomas Fowler Lord of the Manor of Barnsbury (friend of Henry VIII) dies in childbirth. Fowler's lands border those of Canonbury Tower. A look out tower, built for Elizabeth I, was still standing in Mansion House garden in 1655 (some sources say as late as 1861). There are brasses dedicated to Margaret, Robert and Alice Fowler in St Mary's. Sir Thomas Fowler will be one of Ralegh's jurors at his trial. Mansion House (41 Cross Street) the home of the Lord of the Manor of Barnsbury, Deputy Lieutenant for Middlesex, survived until 1845.

1545

Sir Edward North, Chancellor of the Exchequer, who already owns St Mary's Nunnery, buys Charterhouse.

1547

(i) Edward VI doesn't want Canonbury Tower but John Dudley, Duke of Northumberland, does, so Edward swaps it for Tinmouth Priory.

(ii) The Duke of Somerset blows up St John's Priory and uses the stone to build Somerset House in the Strand.

(iii) Barts becomes a teaching hospital. One of its chapels is dedicated to St. Bartholomew the Less to be used by medical staff, patients and visitors (it still is).

1548

Population of Islington is 800. There's a lead mill at the Angel, wind and water mills on the Fleet, oxen and horses pull the plough. Woods are felled for timber.

1549

St Paul's Cathedral takes wagon loads of bones to land it owns near the Artillery training ground in City Road. Dubbed Bonehill, it's now Bunhill.

1550

(i) Barts sends terminal patients to Whittington Hospital. Each takes his own mattress, bolster and sheets.

(ii) The old Hermitage Fields (Rawstorne Street) are bought by Thomas Wilkes.

(iii) Edward VI gives Bride Well Palace to the City Corporation to use as The House of Detention for beggars, vagabonds and tramps which since the closure of nunneries and monasteries have grown dramatically in number. Sir George Baron 'being Mayor of this city, the King gave unto him for the commonality and citizens to be a work house for the poor and idle persons of the city, his house of Bride Well'. After this, all prisons are called Bridewells.

1551

The Lady Mary (demoted from Princess of Wales after her father married Anne Boleyn) moves into St John's Priory. Some sources say her father left it to her in his will, others that half-brother Edward VI inherited it but gave it to her. The procession to St John's consists of: 'Fifty knights afore her and gentlemen in black velvet and chains of gold and more behind each with a peyre of beads in black'.

1553

Treason is afoot in Clerkenwell. John Dudley, Duke of Northumberland of Canonbury Tower asks Sir Edward North to sell him Charterhouse. He wants it for his son Guildford and daughter-in-law, Lady Jane Grey (Edward VI's second cousin) who he intends to get on the throne instead of the Roman Catholic Mary Tudor. Dudley's sons have high aspirations, another son, Robert, hopes to marry Elizabeth I. Dudley buys furniture for Charterhouse which he cheekily stores in St. John's Gate where Mary Tudor is living. Lady Jane, named as his successor by the dying Edward, is about to move into Charterhouse to prepare for her coronation when Dudley is found out. He, Guildford and Lady Jane are executed and their lands including Canonbury Tower revert to the Crown. Astonishingly, even though North signed the paper agreeing Mary be deposed she promotes him to Lord North. Sir William Parr of Charterhouse Square an avid supporter of 'Queen Jane' also sentenced to death is not only pardoned but created Marquis of Northampton. Mary restores some of the damage done to St. John's by Lord Somerset and re-instates the Hospitallers. She invites the Carthusians back to Charterhouse but they opt for Sheen instead.

1557

Queen Mary doesn't want Canonbury Tower so swaps it for Lord Wentworth's Cheney Gate, Westminster.

1558

Lord North invites Elizabeth I to Charterhouse to prepare for her coronation. She stays five days.

1560

The Fortune Theatre opens in Playhouse Yard, Goldyng (Golden) Lane, White Cross Street (Fortune Street).

1561

Elizabeth I refuses to use the roads when she stays for three days with Lord North at Charterhouse so hedges are removed and ditches filled in for her to ride across the fields.

1562

There are 418 Poor Rate payers in Clerkenwell (112 live in Turn Mill Street).

1564

Elizabeth I is in Highbury Fields (Crown Property) inspecting the city's water supply some of which comes from the conduit here (outside present day 14 Highbury Place). Afterwards, she goes hare and fox hunting.

1565 Lord North, almost bankrupted by Elizabeth I two visits, sells Charterhouse to Thomas Howard.

1567

(i) Thomas Howard, duke of Norfolk, brings his third countess to Charterhouse.

(ii) Alice, daughter of Thomas Wilkes who bought Hermitage Fields is almost killed by an arrow. In gratitude for her life she promises to build a school for the children of Islington poor.

1568

Treason is afoot in Clerkenwell. Thomas Howard of Charterhouse, plots to get rid of Elizabeth I. Mary Stuart, Queen of Scots is guarded by Lady Scrope, Margaret Howard (his sister) at Carlisle Castle. Widowered for the third time, he plans to marry her and be Consort of England and Scotland. His sister is the go-between in their courtship. Elizabeth I hears the rumours, moves Mary from Carlisle to Tutbury then Wingfield and on to Coventry. She comes to Charterhouse to stay with her 'dear coz'.

1570

(i) Mary, Queen of Scots, is moved from Coventry to Chatsworth then Sheffield. Elizabeth I summons Thomas Howard to join her at Hampton Court where she asks him to sign a promise that he will have nothing to do with Mary.

(ii) John Spencer a close friend of Elizabeth I buys Canonbury Tower and she visits him on several occasions. Mega rich he already owns Crosby Hall once owned by Richard III. Spencer advises her to take a much stronger line against Catholics.

1571

The Ridolfi Plot. Charterhouse is again centre of world attention. Roberto Ridolfi plans to help Spain and the Netherlands invade Protestant England so that Thomas Howard arch Roman Catholic can marry Mary, Queen of Scots.

1572

(i) Thomas Howard of Charterhouse is, finally and against all Elizabeth I's finer instincts, executed for treason. His lands and properties revert to the Crown. Her advisers want her to execute Queen Mary too but monarchs are God's own anointed so she refuses.

(ii) John Spencer rents Canonbury Tower to Robert Dudley's PPS.

(iii) Inigo Jones is baptised at St. Bartholomew the Great.

1575

Walter Raleigh, war veteran, law student at Inns of Court, moves to Upper Street.

1576

The Theatre, London's first purpose built playhouse, is built in Holy Well Lane. A second, The Curtain, is built nearby the following year.

1579

Elizabeth I gives Edmund Tylney (Censor) St. John's Gate where he will live for thirty years until he dies (1610).

1580

Walter Raleigh of Upper Street is up before the beak. Twice. The first for drunken brawling, the second for fighting on the tennis court.

1581

Elizabeth I banished Robert Dudley from court because he married secretly without her permission. To make him jealous, she invites Walter Raleigh to court. Although hurt and angry, Elizabeth still wants Robert (sweet Robin) near so gives him Shipcote House built by Sir Thomas Lovell in Lower Road (Essex Road) now a Peabody Estate. Dudley loves it and tells Elizabeth that Islington is 'one of the most ancient and best towns in England, next to London'. He raves about its 'cheeses and salt butter, custard curds and whey tarts and other pastry cook delicacies'. In Islington visiting either Dudley, the Fowlers, John Spencer or Raleigh Elizabeth is besieged by 74 'begging rogues' who are thrown in prison.

1582

3000 archers gather in Finsbury Fields for a two day archery competition. Each competitor is given a longbow and four arrows. The winner is escorted home on horseback accompanied by 200 torch bearers.

1584

Elizabeth I gives Raleigh the monopoly 'to make lycences for keeping of taverns and retailing of wines throughout England'. He grants a licence to The Queen's Head, Lower Road in Islington. He may even have built the pub and owned it. The Elizabethan ceiling survived until a landlord installed a slate bed billiard table upstairs and the legs went through. It still has the Elizabethan fireplace. Raleigh may also have converted his house on Upper Street into a pub (The Pied Bull).

1585

Elizabeth I knights Walter Raleigh for colonising a lump of New England (Virginia) and calling it after her, England's virgin queen. She wants to rid London of beggars who now have an option, prison or transportation.

1586

Stage struck William Shakespeare (18) finds lodgings near The Theatre in Holywell Lane. He and the Burbage's are friends until death.

1587

Sir Walter Raleigh is the Queen's personal bodyguard. This means they're inseparable. She buys his ship, the Ark Raleigh, and relaunches it as Ark Royal, flagship of her fleet.

1588

(i) The Artillery Company (City Road) fights in the Armada.

(ii) The King's Head in Upper Street is rebuilt.

1589

Lord Compton of Bruce Castle in Tottenham goes to Canonbury Tower to borrow money from Sir John Spencer. He and Eliza, Spencer's only child, fall in love.

1592

Ralph Agas draws the first map of London. It shows Islington 'on the waye to St Alban' and includes 'Schmyt Fielde, St Bartholomew, White Cross Street, Red Cross Street, Goldinge Lane, Olde Street, Chis Well Street,

Charterhouse and Canonbury Tower'. The map shows windmills and archers in the fields.

1593

The earl of Cumberland, who captained the Queen's ship Elizabeth 'Bonaventura' in the Spanish Armada is tenant of Charterhouse for two years. One of her favourites, she lent him her ship 'The Golden Lion' for ten raids on Spain all of which were spectacularly unsuccessful.

1595

(i) William Shakespeare is with Tylney the censor at St John's Gate with his seven shillings fee to licence Romeo and Juliet. Once passed fit for human consumption he loads his props on a boat and sails down the Fleet to The Globe on the Thames.

(ii) A Gate and Gate House is built leading to the nave of St Bartholomew the Great.

1596

The Corporation of London takes over Smithfield Market and Bartholomew Fair.

1597

Shakespeare writes *Henry IV*. He has Sir John Oldcastle, Henry's drinking partner rollicking in the brothels in Turnmill Street. There is uproar. Locals object to their hero being depicted as a figure of fun and complain to the censor who orders Shakespeare to take the character out. Shakespeare substitutes Sir John Falstaff.

1598

(i) Stowe's Survey of London includes Charterhouse Square, Cow Lane Bridge and Chick Lane Bridge over the River of Wells, the Clerks Well, Fagges Well, Gode Well, Loder's Well, Rad Well, the Walbrook and the River of Wells.

(ii) Dame Alice (Wilkes) Owen starts a school at the Angel to educate the children of Islington's poor.

1599

(i) Sir John Spencer noshes up Canonbury Tower. His chimney pieces, ceilings and panelling are still there. His daughter Eliza elopes with Lord Compton of Bruce Castle. Their first baby, a son, Spencer, has Elizabeth I as sponsor (Godparent). Their second child, a daughter, is born in Canonbury Tower and baptised in St Mary's in Upper Street.

(ii) The Red Bull Theatre opens in Woodbridge Street.

(iii) Sir Thomas Chaloner the Younger (son of the diplomat) of Clerkenwell, a naturalist, finds alum on his land in Guisborough Yorkshire.

1600

(i) Bad plague year. 322 Islingtonians die (yearly average is 47)

(ii) The Long Causeway (the high pavement) is built in Upper Street (it's still there).

1603

Elizabeth I gives Charterhouse to 'my good Thomas' (Sir Thomas Howard, second son of the Howard executed for treason). This Howard is no traitor; he commanded her ship The Golden Lion in the Armada, was knighted for gallantry on board The Ark Royal and made Admiral of the Fleet. She pays her fourth and last visit to Charterhouse just before she dies and makes him Lord Howard of Walden. Thomas Howard invites her successor James I (age 37) to Charterhouse to prepare for his coronation on the last lap from Scotland; he rests at The King's Head, Upper Street. Is he the 'king' on the pub sign? He stays four days in Charterhouse and in the Great Chamber, one of the finest Elizabethan rooms in existence, where Liz danced in her young days; one hundred and thirty-three receive a Knighthood. Well out of favour, Walter Ralegh is put in the Tower where he stays until James needs him in 1616.

1604

The King loves the theatre even more than Elizabeth did. The Prince's Men rehearse at The Fortune Theatre and The Queen's Men at The Red Bull, Sekforde Street. James knights Edmund Tylney, the Censor, and asks him to bring the season forward from Boxing Day to November which puts Tylney in a tizz at St John's Gate. Theatre companies are falling over each other rehearsing. Will Shakespeare is so impressive the King gives his company a royal patent, a very Royal Shakespeare Company indeed. The season opens with Shakespeare's *Othello* at Whitehall. In fact Shakespeare's company is presenting nearly all the plays. The King's Men are putting on *The Merry Wives of Windsor, Measure for Measure, The Comedy of Errors, Loves Labours Lost., Henry V* and *The Merchant of Venice* all before *Twelfth Night*. The Queen's Men (his wife Anne also adores theatre) are putting on a play, the Boys Company at Blackfriars another, there are two amateur companies at The Gate rehearsing a masque for the Earl of Pembroke and Ben Jonson is rehearsing a masque starring the Queen with scenery designed by Inigo Jones. It takes Tylney and four assistants twenty days just to get the costumes ready.

1605

(i) The Chancellor of the Exchequer rents Canonbury Tower.

(ii) Guy Fawkes, planning The Gunpowder Plot, visits his ally Thomas Sleep in St Peter Street Clerkenwell. 7 November. The Calendar of State Papers. 'From Salisbury House to Mr Percival. Informs him of divers houses of recusants in St John St amongst them Mr Thomas Sleep. Guy Johnson (alias Fawkes) is often at Sleep's house'

1610

(i) Sir John Spencer, dies. Lord Compton (through Eliza, Sir John's daughter) inherits his vast fortune of £800,000 and goes (temporarily) mad. All his life he has been in debt and can't immediately adjust to wealth. He and Elizabeth leave Canonbury Tower to live at his country seat, Castle Ashby, Northampton. Elizabeth doesn't know it but fate decrees she will be back one day as an impoverished grandmother.

(ii) Justices of the Peace for Middlesex (London is in Middlesex until 1900) a huge county which reaches as far as Stepney, get brassed off with holding court in upstairs rooms of The Castle Inn St John Street. Sir Baptist Hicks money lender, rich mercer, Viscount Camden, MP and JP for Middlesex says if James I donates land he will build, at his own expense, a purpose built court house. He asks for a derelict piece of land in St John Street yards from Smithfield Market to build a hall to administer law and order. James agrees and grants a license to build.

1611

(i) James I gives the manor of Highbury to his son Henry, Prince of Wales.

(ii) Sir Henry Mildmay, Revenue Commissioner, buys 44 acres of Newington and calls his home, The Park.

(iii) Thomas Howard sells Charterhouse to Thomas Sutton who converts it into a public school and old folks home.

(iv) The school is here for three hundred years until 1872 when it moves to Godalming. The old folks home is still there.

1612

When Sir Edmund Tylney dies, James I gives St. John's Gate to Sir Roger Wilbrahim (one of his boyfriends). The new censor relocates to Black Friars, South Bank, where Shakespeare's Globe is doing a roaring trade. Roaring is just about right. Soon it will burn down.

1613

(i) Hicks Hall, London's first purpose built Court House, opens in St John Street. Miles from London are measured from here so Clerkenwell becomes famous all over Britain.

(ii) The population of London is growing fast and water is scarce. Wells not closed during Henry VIII's religious purge (he closed all 'holy' wells) have dried up as have ponds and rivers. Hugh Myddelton, Welsh MP, brother of Sir Thomas Myddelton MP, Lord Mayor of London, supervises six hundred labourers as they cut by hand a thirty eight mile canal, four foot deep, ten foot wide, eighty foot above sea level between Ware in Hertfordshire and Islington. It takes five years. One hundred and fifty bridges are built. In some places the river needs an aqueduct so the venture is ambitious and expensive. Water from St. Chad's Well and Am Well in Hertfordshire is supplemented by the river Lea. Myddelton, though not poor, doesn't have the kind of money needed but as MP for Chirk North Wales and goldsmith to King James he has rich friends in high places (Dame Alice Wilkes Owen is one) so knows he can raise it. Myddelton runs out of money but James I who has a Royal estate and hunting lodge at Theobalds, Hertfordshire, watches progress and puts up half the money. Royalty, as ever, gives the venture prestige so raising the rest is not a problem. Myddelton's family owns coal pits in Wales so he knows all about water extraction and is a first class engineer. Ware, twenty miles away as the crow flies, is one hundred and twelve feet higher than Finsbury where the river ends so water follows a one hundred foot contour line for forty miles. The drop of five inches every mile means it doesn't flow very fast as it meanders through Broxbourne, Cheshunt, Enfield, Wood Green, Hornsey, Haringey, Holloway, Islington, Finsbury, Clerkenwell on to the City. Land owners along the way are financially appeased. Rich Islingtonians pay for the river to be routed past their houses. It runs down Asteys Row past the Fowler house, Cross Street diagonally across Lower Street (Essex Road) to Colebrooke Row and on to Rosebery Avenue.

(iii) Sir Hugh Myddelton's New River opens. His friend, Dame Alice Owen, opens her school on the river just before she dies. She's buried in St.Mary's.

1615

(i) A prison is built in Sans Walk. There will be one here for over three hundred years until 1890.

(ii) Sir Francis Bacon moves into Canonbury Tower

(iii) Dr. William Harvey of Barts discovers the circulation of blood.

(iv) The first pupil is enrolled at Charterhouse Public School.

1618

William Compton, earl of Northampton is created a Lord. He re-names Bruce Castle Lordship House.

1621

Sir Francis Bacon of Canonbury Tower is created Viscount St. Albans three days before he's found guilty of corruption on twenty-three counts, stripped of office, banished from Court, fined £40k and put in the Tower.

1625

(i) Sir Thomas Coventry, Lord Keeper of the Great Seal, Solicitor General, Recorder of London, Attorney General, MP Droitwich moves into Canonbury Tower.

(ii) The steeple on the nuns medieval St James Church in Clerkenwell collapses and is rebuilt.

1627

The Red Bull Theatre Sekforde Street starts putting on plays by Shakespeare but they're so bad they're booed off stage. The Company goes back to showing comedies.

1630

Lord William Compton, Eliza Spencer's husband, of Bruce Castle Tottenham, dines at Whitehall then dies after swimming in the Thames. His son, Spencer, succeeds to the Earldom and sells Lordship House.

Henry, Lord Coleraine, Lord of the Manor of Tottenham moves in and uses its original name Bruce Castle. He builds a family vault there where he is buried (1708).

1633

Red Bull Theatre Sekforde Street tries another crowd puller. It employs female actors, the first theatre in Britain to do so.

1635

James Stanley KB, MP, Lord Strange, earl of Derby moves into Canonbury Tower. A Royalist, he is executed by Oliver Cromwell and dubbed The Martyr Earl.

1638

(i) The Angel Inn is rebuilt with a double galleried coach yard which doubles as a theatre.

(ii) The Corporation of London tries to change the ancient name of Smithfield Market to Newgate Street Market. It clearly never caught on.

1641

(i) The Crown opens on Clerkenwell Green.

(ii) The Artillery Company moves to City Road.

(iii) Charles I gives Highbury to Sir Allen Apsley, loyal Royalist leader.

(iv) Earl of Aylesbury builds a mansion on the remains of St John's Priory and calls it Aylesbury House. He uses the crypt of the Hospitallers church as a wine cellar. The Aylesbury's own the property until 1706.

1642

(i) Oliver Cromwell stays in Clerkenwell Close at the home of fellow republicans, James and Sir Thomas Chaloner. Charles I has taken their valuable alum mines in Yorkshire. Cromwell fortifies St John Street and Goswell Road against Royalists.

(ii) Lord (Spencer) Compton (42) who spent his early years in Canonbury Tower dies in battle fighting Cromwell's New Model Army. Cromwell deprives the family of Compton Wynyates so the family return to Canonbury Tower where Spencer's parents fell in love and where his sister was born.

(iii) It's thought that Franz Hals' 'The Laughing Cavalier' (one of the most famous paintings in the world now worth many millions) is Sir William Halton (Halton Road) a rich Islington landowner and Royalist (he also had a portrait painted by Van Dyck). Despising showiness, Puritan Parliamentarians wore their hair short so were nicknamed 'Roundheads'. Royalists such as Halton celebrated courtly flamboyance so were called Cavaliers. Londoners tend to support parliament.

1644

Islington: Home of the Quakers. George Fox, founder, arrives in Clerkenwell. The word 'Quaker' a term of derision came about after he called upon those in authority to tremble before the Lord. He preaches against war at the Meeting House in St John Street and against Calvin who believes in pre-destiny, saying we can be saved from ourselves. He despises all formal religions and goes to church, which he calls steeple houses, to interrupt sermons. Always in and out of prison, he makes missionary journeys to Scotland, Ireland, Holland, North America and the West Indies but comes back to Clerkenwell to die.

His followers bought Banner Street cemetery for a Quaker Burial Ground and Bunhill Meeting House, 21 Coleman Street, Bunhill Row. Fox is buried in Janner Street, White Cross Street, Bunhill Row.

1649

(i) Treason is afoot in Clerkenwell. Again. Sir Thomas Chaloner of Clerkenwell Close signs Charles I death warrant.

(ii) The White Conduit House (later The Penny Farthing Pub) opens for business the day Charles is beheaded.

(iii) Izaac Walton retires to Clerkenwell Green.

1650

Highbury Woods, the last bit of the Great Forest of Middlesex, are chopped down.

1651

Cromwell is a Governor of Charterhouse. 'We the said committee do likewise think that the Arms of the late King standing above the gates be forthwith pulled down and defaced and that the arms of the Commonwealth be put up in the same place'. Cromwell was wrong; they were not the Arms of Charles I but of his father James I. A hundred years before, Henry VIII hanged human arms on the gate, those of Prior John Houghton.

1653

(i) A teacher and fervent monarchist from Islington, Mr Vowel, (truly) who plotted to kill Cromwell is hanged at Charing Cross where he is arrested.

(ii) Cromwell dismisses Sir Thomas Chaloner, fellow regicide, erstwhile landlord and friend, from Parliament calling him an incompetent drunk but returns the alum mines in Yorkshire to him. Alum was used as a base in skin whiteners

(iii) The Artillery Company is appointed official escort of the Lord Mayor

(iv) A son is born to the exiled Lord Compton at Canonbury Tower.

(v) Izaac Walton publishes *The Compleat Angler*. The language he uses is, wisely, Puritan, heaven forfend anyone should enjoy anything.

1654

Lord Compton is forced to sell Crosby Hall and take out a mortgage on Canonbury Tower. He forms The Sealed Knot a secret society to get rid of Cromwell.

1655

Life's no fun under Cromwell. Islingtonians are used to theatres, brothels, bear baiting, gambling dens and numerous places of entertainment. There's no monarchy so no Court, no House of Lords so no aristos to laugh at. Swearing is a fineable offence and adultery a capital one. Each district had a Soldier Major General enforcing Sabbath Day; Gambling, drinking, racing, cock fighting, dancing around the maypole and celebrating Christmas were forbidden. There are no writers, musicians, painters, concert halls or galleries. In Grub Street Clerkenwell (now the Barbican) a club is launched determined to have some fun, The Farting Club meets every week 'to pyson the neighbourhood with noisome crepitations' as the members attempt to out fart each other.

1656

(i) William D'Avenant of Rutland House, Charterhouse Square (who says he's Shakespeare's illegitimate son) puts on England's first opera.

(ii) Parishioners buy St James, Clerkenwell.

(iii) Four houses are built on Newington Green (now the oldest terrace in London).

1660

(i) 9 October. Hicks Hall St John Street. The trial takes place of '29 Regicides, murderers of his most sacred majesty Charles I. This day the bloody murderers of the late king are removed to the common prison of the county to be tried at the Sessions House St John Street'. James Chaloner died in Holland where he was hiding. His brother, Sir Thomas committed suicide. An Islington drayman, Colonel Okey in Cromwell's New Model Army is brought back from Holland and hanged.

(ii) Charles II gives William D'Avenant a patent to run a theatre and builds a country home for Nell Gwynn, the favourite of his thirty-three mistresses, on the banks of the Fleet near present day King's Cross.

1661

(i) Islington: Home of *Paradise Lost* and *Paradise Regained*. John Milton, 54, blind at 43 through glaucoma marries for the third time. Elizabeth Minshull is 24. The couple move to 124 Bunhill Row from where he publishes *Paradise Lost* and dictates *Paradise Regained* to his daughter Deborah. Civil servant under Cromwell (Latin Secretary to Council of State and Censor of Publications) his books are burnt after the Restoration by the public hangman and he is put in prison. His friend Andrew Marvell poetic MP petitioned to get him released. In 1643 Milton married Mary Powell sixteen years his junior who died in childbirth after their fourth child. The first, Anne, was born disabled, his son John died young but Mary and Deborah thrived. His second wife who he married in 1656, Catherine Woodcock, twenty years younger died two years later and their only child died young. Every day he dictates forty lines of *Paradise Lost* to Deborah but in the 1700s Dr Johnson was appalled to find that Deborah's daughter, Elizabeth, Milton's granddaughter, had never been taught to read and was having to beg to eat. He and David Garrick put on a Benefit night for her.

(ii) Sir Arthur Hesilrige/Haselrig MP (hero of Cromwell's wars) escaped hanging but has, naturally, many enemies among the nobility. On his way home to Holloway from the House of Commons he is attacked by the Earl of Stamford in Perpoole Lane Clerkenwell. He dies later the same year in the Tower.

1662

The Duke of Newcastle, fervent Royalist, spent £1m in service to the monarchy but, treated badly after the Restoration, retires from court and demolishes what remains of St Mary's Nunnery, Clerkenwell Close, to build Newcastle House. He is Ben Jonson's patron as is his Duchess, thirty years his junior (Mad Madge). Her grand black and silver coach has footmen in velvet uniform. After her death she lay in state at Newcastle House from 15 December until 7 January before being buried in Westminster Abbey. Newcastle House will survive until 1793 when James Carr demolishes it to build a row of houses.

1663

(i) Samuel Pepys frequents St James Church (he desires a woman in the congregation), The King's Head in Upper Street, The Mother Redcap in Holloway Road and The Red Bull Theatre, Woodbridge Street.

(ii) Turnpikes are erected to collect tolls to mend the roads.

(iii) The Red Bull Theatre Woodbridge Street closes.

1664

2,061 live in Islington, 20,281 in Clerkenwell.

1665

Worst plague in living memory. Many city survivors move to Islington and never return.

1666

The Great Fire of London. Many survivors build shanty towns here and never return.

1667

The Act of Uniformity demands we must, within a five mile radius of London, literally, sing from the same hymn book. Non-Conformists move outside the radius to Newington Green.

1672

The most famous prophet in Western history wrote in a secret mediaeval, occult code, The Green Language. Dr Garencières, Clerkenwell Close, physician to the French ambassador translates and publishes *Nostradamus* who, it's said, predicted events eight hundred years in the future including the French Revolution, First and Second World Wars and the Spanish Civil War.

1675

(i) Daniel Foe (he added the 'De' in prison when he was forty) is enrolled at Charles Morton's Dissenters Academy, Newington Green.

(ii) The Bethlem (Bedlam) Lunatic Hospital is built in Moor Fields (now Finsbury Circus).

1678

Thomas Britton of Jerusalem Passage starts London's first musical society.

1682

Edmund Halley, mentor to Isaac Newton, moves to Islington where he stays fourteen years. He builds an observatory and discovers the comet (and its return in 1759) named in his honour.

1683

(i) Anne, second daughter of the exiled James II, marries George of Denmark.

(ii) Sadler's Wells Musicke House. Dick Sadler's labourers (he's a Highways Engineer) re-discover two wells once owned by St John's Priory, filled in by Henry VIII. He moves his theatre here from St John's Gate. More than three hundred years later, a music house is still here.

1685

(i) James, Duke of York, sues Titus Oates for libel at Hicks Hall.

(ii) Thousands of Huguenots hounded out of France for being Protestants come to Clerkenwell.

1687

Daniel Foe's first child, Daniel, is baptised in St James, Clerkenwell.

1691

The first ever salute over a grave is at St James, Clerkenwell when Sir William Wood, Queens Archer, is buried with full honours. Three flights of whistling arrows are released.

1697

William Hogarth is christened in St Bartholomew the Great. The font is still there.

1700

(i) London is now the worlds largest city (Pop. 600,000). 25% depend on the Port of London for their livelihood which handles 80% of the country's imports and 70% of its exports.

(ii) The ancient buildings of St Bartholomew's, St John's and St Mary's are in multi-use as accommodation and small businesses

(iii) Waves of plagues and fires still rage within the City walls and encourage more people to settle in Islington. As the hoi polloi move in, so the toffs move out to the rapidly developing west end.

(iv) At Bell Brewery Shoreditch, Ralph Harwood calls his new beers: entire butt (a thick dark brew blended from three different beers) pale ale, brown ale and stale ale. Stale ale was so cheap Smithfield porters could afford to drink copious amounts so it was dubbed 'porter'. Another darker, thicker beer, much 'stouter' was called stout. Stout, brewed in Dublin (1918) became Guinness named after its brewer.

1702

(i) London's first daily newspaper *The Daily Courant* is printed near the Fleet Bridge.

(ii) Rev. Isaac Watts is Minister of Newington Green Non-Conformist Chapel where he stays fifty years until his death. He writes six hundred hymns here among them some of England's most famous including: *When I Survey The Wondrous Cross, Joy To The World, Jesus Shall Reign Where'er The Sun* and *Oh God Our Help In Ages Past.*

1703

(i) Defoe's *Private Eye* style *The Shortest Way with Dissenters*' is welcomed and taken very seriously by Queen Anne who hates Dissenters. Exposed as a send up, he is fined, imprisoned in Newgate and pilloried for irreverence. Being a local hero passers by pelt him not with stones or rotten fruit as is the custom but with flowers. Others visit to drink his health. While in prison, Foe writes *Hymn to the Pillory* and to while away the time, starts his own newspaper *The Review*. He writes the entire paper himself and makes up all the news. He decides Foe is far too pedestrian a moniker for a man of genius so adds the 'de'.

(ii) On his rounds in Warwick Court, Thomas Britton the coalie, is hailed from the studio window of the painter, Wollaston, a member of Britton's Musick Club, who recognises Britton's 'cry' out of all the others competing for business in the busy street below and calls him in to paint his portrait. The portrait is in the NPG. It is not on display but can be seen by appointment.

(iii) St Bartholomew the Less is built as a parish church for patients at Bart's hospital. Classical style with Ionic pilasters and broken pediment.

(iv) William Hogarth's father opens a coffee shop in St John's Gate.

(v) Daniel Foe having done just about everything else embarks on yet another career. He tries his hand at writing and proves to be very good at it, so good that by the time he dies he will have published over 250 works. Because of strong public feeling against William of Orange he begins with a satire, *The True-Born Englishman*, which derides the idea of the purity of Englishness. The monarch is well pleased.

1706

(i) Defoe writes another satire, this time on the divine right of kings or not.

(ii) St Johns Church, empty and neglected, is leased to Non-Conformists. Bad move.

1707

The Act of Union unites the Kingdoms of Scotland and England. The Scots feel betrayed. Defoe goes to Scotland to spy for England.

1708

(i) Bishop Burnet retires to 36 (renumbered 44) St. John Square to write *History of the Reformation*. The mansion, inherited from his wife, has two storeys, three gables, fourteen square windows on the front, a forecourt with trees and shrubs and large grounds at the rear. Steps lead up to a portico supported by Tuscan columns. Burnet gives Sunday evening lectures attended by nobility including the Dukes of Newcastle (who lives around the corner in Clerkenwell Close) and Marlborough.

(ii) Joseph Addison becomes a MP. He founds The Kit Kat Club (which meets at the house of Mr Christopher Cat) with Richard Steele.

(iii) 1 Jan. Defoe takes his baby son Daniel to St James Church in Clerkenwell to be christened.

(iv) Red Lion Street, after the local tavern, is developed by Simon Michell. 54 and 55 are Islington's oldest surviving houses. No 55 still has the original shop window with fluted pilasters. Both are clearly built before the Fire Act of 1709. The windows are flush with the brickwork. Under the new Act doors and windows must be recessed at least four inches from the front of the building. The Statute sets a fashion which emulates outside London.

Other countries may have finer palaces, larger cathedrals and town halls grander but England built the finest domestic housing.

1709

(i) Richard Steele starts *The Tatler* with Joseph Addison.

(ii) Dr Henry Sacheverell. a High Church Tory MP hates all Non-Conformists and rejects the concept of religious toleration as does Queen Anne. At Southwark Cathedral he delivers two bitter sermons accusing the government of jeopardising the established Church of England by going soft on Dissenters.

1710

(i) Sacheverell is tried and impeached in the House of Commons for his outburst and suspended for three years which makes him a martyr. Defoe supports his impeachment in his *Review*. Thousands of Sacheverell supporters go on the rampage burning down Non Confomist chapels among them St John's Church in St. John's Square used as a Presbyterian Meeting House. Bishop Burnet who lives in the Square while writing the history of the Reformation watches it being torched and on the reports the riots.

(ii) Water is no longer pumped at New River Head by wind (mill), horse power is used instead.

(iii) Steele writes about the Fleet river in *The Tatler*: The filth of all hues and odours seem to tell what street they sailed from by their sight and smell, sweepings from butchers stalls, dung guts and blood, drowned puppies, all drowned in mud, dead cats and turnip tops come tumbling down the flood. The rich build latrines over narrow parts of the Fleet.

1711

Addison and Steele start *The Spectator* to take place of Steele's *Tatler*. It appears daily, readership is aimed at London upper middle class. Lady Montagu is a contributor. They invent the Spectator Club led by Sir Roger de Coverley (possibly the pre-cursor of Dickens' Pickwick Club). Dr Johnson was a great admirer of the paper.

1712

Satirist Ned Ward, publisher of *London Spy: Sketches of London Life* opens a pub in Red Bull Yard opposite Jerusalem Passage (accessed via Aylesbury Street). In 'British Wonders' he writes: 'The Bulls and Bears, Old Dung hills, Night-men, Slaughterers Jayls, Butchers Dogs and Hogs that dwell In sweet St James Clerkenwell'. He becomes close friends with Thomas Britton and attends his musical concerts likening the players in the tiny cramped room to 'sweaty dancers at a Buttocks Ball'. After Britton's death Ward with his buddy, type setter

William Caslon arrange a sale of his effects to help his widow.

1713

(i) Richard Steele, who will be knighted in 1715, founds *The Guardian* newspaper.

(ii) His suspension over, Queen Anne gives Sacheverell, St Andrews Holborn, a rich living as a reward.

(iii) Defoe's subversive *Review* is suppressed and he is prosecuted for writing treasonable pamphlets.

(iv) Thomas Tompion of Clerkenwell, father of English watch making, is buried in Westminster Abbey. He made the first English watch with a balance spring, clocks for The Royal Observatory at Greenwich and the famous clock in The Bath Pump Rooms.

1714

(i) The White Lion near The Angel Inn is rebuilt on the site of the 1500s Wyte Lion Inn. It's still the favourite of drovers

(ii) Church Cottage is built for the sexton of St Mary's in Upper Street (still there). The sexton is in charge of the fabric and contents of church building. In times of need he doubles as gravedigger.

(iii) The Duke of Buckingham nominates John Wesley for a free place at Charterhouse. One of fifty boys age 10 to 14, he writes to his father every day. John Wesley, born in Lincolnshire, is the fifteenth of Susannah and the Reverend Samuel Wesley's nineteen children. His maternal and paternal grandfathers both Puritan ministers give up their CofE livings rather than conform to the official prayer book. Part of the old Wellesley family, Wesley will grow up labelled a crank because of his revolutionary doctrine that everyone can be saved through faith alone. Wesley lived fifty-six of his eighty-eight years in Islington. John Pepusch, later to become famous or infamous as the composer of *The Beggar's Opera*, is the organist at Charterhouse. In adulthood Wesley will revisit Pepusch and his old school often.

(iv) Queen Anne dies. Her successor, George I, Elector of Hanover, great-grandson of James I, is King. Handel who visited England in 1710 and 1712 now settles in London. He plays the organ and harpsichord at Britton's musical evenings in Clerkenwell some Thursdays. The Duchess of Queensbury is also a regular visitor as is composer and friend Pepusch. In one tiny room assemble the wit, genius and beauty of London. Thomas Britton, the coalie, dies and is buried in St James churchyard. Although 70, his death is sad and completely unnecessary. Sir Roger L'Estrange JP Middlesex who often performs at Britton's Thursday evening music club literally has Britton frightened to death. He decided to play a practical joke on Britton. He hires a ventriloquist to order him go down on his knees and recite The Lord's Prayer. Britton dies four days later. Sir Hans Sloane buys Britton's large collection of rare books and manuscripts. They will form the nucleus of The British Museum.

(v) Defoe is in trouble again, this time for libelling Lord Annesley.

(vi) The Riot Act is passed as a direct result of the Sacheverell riots. Considering the riots which come to the same square not long after, no-one, clearly, took a scrap of notice.

1716

(i) William Caslon friend of Thomas Britton, founder of the famous metal typeface, sets up shop in Chiswell Street.

(ii) Descendants of Welsh immigrants, London Celts in Clerkenwell, launch Loyal Society of Ancient Britons.

1717

(i) Joseph Addison, anarchic by nature, yearns to be part of the establishment. Although temperamentally unsuited, finally manages it. He is made Secretary of State.

(ii) Ned Ward writes about 'all the stinks that rise together from Hockley in the Hole in sultry weather'. Hockley in the Hole, the bed of the Fleet river, is now a slum.

1718

(i) The well loved pre-Reformation nunnery church, re-dedicated to St James the Less following the Reformation, over five hundred years old, is falling to bits. Structurally unsound is the official term. Discussions take place about pulling it down and building a new one.

(ii) America is the dumping ground for the transportation of UK undesirables.

1719

(i) Canonbury Tower is now a lodging house.

(ii) Joseph Addison dies. He is buried in Westminster Abbey. Richard Steele will live another 10 years.

(iii) Age 60, Defoe writes *Robinson Crusoe*, the first great English novel. He met Alexander Selkirk, a shipwrecked mariner whose experiences Defoe embellished using buckets of artistic licence. The fabrication was believed because people knew that Defoe met Selkirk.

1720

(i) 5 November Bonfire (Guy Fawkes) Night. An accident at Brock's Fireworks, Islington Road (St. John Street) kills owner John Brock and his daughter. They were buried in St James Clerkenwell.

(ii) Cheap corn means cheap gin. Alcoholism is now a serious social problem. One day William Hogarth will paint 'Gin Lane' to shock the establishment. Short, stocky and plain Hogarth a Londoner through and through adored England and loathed all foreigners. Longing to be an artist, because of his father's bankruptcy was instead apprenticed to a silver plater and engraver.

(iii) The Vicar of St Marys in Upper Street is Revd. George Carey. One day a young curate there of that name will be appointed Archbishop of Canterbury.

(iv) Daniel Defoe publishes a sequel to *Robinson Crusoe*.

(v) The Rates Books show a Mr Crosse, brewer, as lessee of the Clerks Well.

(vi) William Caslon moves to Helmet Row and runs a print shop there for 60 years. He created which is still used today. See: http://en.wikipedia.org/wiki/Caslon

(vii) John Wesley leaves Charterhouse for Oxford to study theology.

1721

Albion Place Clerkenwell is the home of Mr Pinchbeck, watch and clock maker who invents an alloy which looks like gold. Pinchbeck is the name afterward given to an alloy of 80 per cent copper and 20 per cent zinc a substitute for bronze and gold used to make cheap watch cases and imitation jewellery. The name Pinchbeck came to mean anything counterfeit, cheap or flashy. He also makes musical/astronomical clocks and boxes, Musical Automata, which simulate flutes, minuets, jigs, psalms, tunes from the opera and bird song. They are bought by small country churches with no organist. The Clerkenwell clock face is so popular French and German clocks are sent here to have them put on.

1722

(i) Daniel Defoe publishes *Journal of the Plague Year* and *Moll Flanders*.

(ii) Jack Sheppard, the famous highwayman, escapes from The New Prison in Sans Walk Clerkenwell. As an apprentice, young Jack is lured away from the straight and narrow by his girl friend Edgeworth Bess and her friend Polly Maggott. They are having far more fun outside the law than he is within it so he joined their den of thieves. During the course of his very short life, Sheppard, London's best loved and most popular of highwaymen is imprisoned five times and escapes four.

In prison here with Edgeworth Bess he filed off his fetters and the window bars and climbed 25 feet below by tying blankets together. Walls around prison were 22 feet high so they climbed over the gates.

(iii) There is no stone around London, it's so scarce it's brought from Kent. To meet increasing demand, Elizabeth Coade, a chemist, who lives in Charterhouse Square, improves on a lapsed patent for artificial stone which she patents as Coade Stone. Something similar was being used by two 'men of Lambeth' but didn't have the 'added something' of the Coade family. The Coade's become very rich. Coade Stone, cheap to manufacture, proved more durable than natural stone. The secret died with the last of the family and the Stone resisted all attempts at analysis until 1996. Elizabeth Coade's secret formula was: 60-70% Ball Clay, 10% crushed soda lime glass, 10% grog (finely crushed previously fired debris), 5-10% crushed flint and 5-10% fine quartz.

1723

(i) Sir George Colebrooke buys Highbury Manor.

(ii) Simon Michell, a local JP demolishes the derelict St. John's Church burnt out in the Sacheverell Riots. He builds a new church and sells it to Queen Anne's Commissioners who re-consecrate it as the Parish Church of St John Clerkenwell.

1724

(i) Benjamin Franklin, printer, teetotal and a genius, arrives in Clerkenwell from America. Here to buy typeface from William Caslon he is unable to return because his money and letters of introduction have been stolen. He gets a job in Samuel Palmer's Printing Works, Bartholomew Close (the old Lady Chapel) but it takes him two years to save enough to go home. Franklin enjoys London but is taken aback at how lazy Londoners were. He loves the theatre and is a friend of Henry Fielding, Hans Sloane, Thomas Paine and William Caslon.

(ii) Jack Shepherd is up before the beak again. This time he has gone too far and is sentenced to death at the Old Bailey. He awaits his fate in Newgate on the third floor above the gate house hand-cuffed and manacled to floor. Not wanting to disappoint his friends he manages to escape but is caught on Finchley Common and finds himself back in Newgate. This time he escapes by climbing up the chimney. Celebrating his luck with a jar too far, he is caught again. People pay huge amounts of money to stare at him while he is on Death Row at Newgate in the condemned cell. He is hanged at Tyburn in front of 200,000 spectators, many of them fans. Apprentices and journeymen are given a day's holiday.

1725

(i) William Caslon type founder, opens a workshop at 5, Helmet Row.

(ii) Daniel Defoe, who gave the world a very scary footprint, (*Robinson Crusoe*) hides from his creditors in a rented bedsit in Ropemaker Street. Using the pseudonym, Andrew Morton, he dies here six years later in 1731.

1727

John Wilkes, a one man Magna Carta, is born in St James Court, St John Square, Clerkenwell. He will become local, national and international hero for proving that a warrant for arrest must have your name on it, championing freedom of the press and for championing the cause of the American colonists by giving them their slogan 'No Tax Without Representation'.

1728

Local composer John Pepusch, organist at Charterhouse, writes the score for *The Beggars Opera* and becomes embroiled in a public outcry arising from the great and the good. The anti-opera produces an instant pop song 'Over the hills and far away'. The hero Captain Macheath a romanticised highwayman and homme fatal is based on local hero Jack Sheppard. John Gay, John Rich and John Pepusch are accused of causing juvenile delinquency when highway robbery increased after the opera with copycat hold-ups. Two hundred years later the opera will inspire Bertolt Brecht and Kurt Weill's *The Threepenny Opera* which also features Macheath and Polly Peachum.

1731

Edward Cave of Highbury Place introduces the term 'magazine' into publishing when he founds *The Gentleman's Magazine* at St John's Gate. It survives until the 1914-18 war.

1733

(i) Dick Turpin and Claude Duval famous highwaymen, rob coaches in Hornsey Lane.

(ii) Colley Cibber, poet laureate, moves to Colebrooke Row.

(iii) Princess Amelia and Princess Caroline, daughters of George II visit Islington Spa almost every day in the summer.

1735

Eustace Budgell, Joseph Addison's cousin to whom he was close, lives in fashionable Coldbath Square. He writes for *The Spectator* signing his pieces 'X'. Having lost all his money in the 'South Sea Bubble' affair he was publicly disgraced after being found guilty of attempted fraud. He hires a Thames boatman and jumps into the Thames. You do wonder. Did the boatman get paid first?

1737

(i) Alexander Cruden of Camden Passage publishes the Concordance To The Bible.

(ii) Dr Johnson starts writing for Cave's *The Gentleman's Magazine* in St John's Gate.

1738

(i) The King's Printer, William Caslon of funky font fame, moves from Helmet Row to Chiswell Street where he stays twenty-eight years until he dies world famous. Thanks to his friend Benjamin Franklin, The American Declaration of Human Rights is printed using his fonts.

(ii) Charles Wesley, brother of John, assistant curate at St Mary's Upper Street writes *Hark The Herald Angels Sing*.

1739

C of E, St Mary's in Upper Street launches Methodism, the largest Protestant denomination in the world when it refuses to let John Wesley use the pulpit. He is forced to preach in a disused gun foundry in City Road. One day millions of Methodists all over the world will celebrate his birthday. He will have hospitals, schools, colleges, churches and missions named after him.

1741

George Dance (the Younger) architect in embryo is born to architect George Dance the Elder (who designed Mansion House) in Chiswell Street

1743

Henry Carey, illegitimate son of the Marquis of Halifax, resident musician at Sadler's Wells, commits suicide in Great Warner Street. He wrote the words for the English national anthem *God Save The King* and *Sally* (made famous by Gracie Fields).

1744

The world's first Methodist conference is held in City Road.

1745

John Wesley's friend, John Horton, buys 25 Highbury Place.

1747

William Hogarth paints 'Stage Coach at the Angel Inn' Islington.

1750

(i) The old river Fleet is now an open sewer.

(ii) Whitbread's Brewery opens in Chiswell Street. It becomes the UK's leading food drinks empire and will one day own the chains Brewer's Fayre, Wayside Inns, Hanrahans, Cafe Rouge, TGI Friday, Pizza Hut, Marriott, Country Club, Travel Inn, IPA, Flowers, Boddington, Murphy's, Heineken, Stella Artois and the David Lloyd Gym chain.

1751

St Mary's Church Upper Street is rebuilt. It will survive until WWII.

1754

'The Parr's Head' is built on the corner of Upper Street and Cross Street ('Old Parr's Head'). His connection, if any, with Islington is not known nor why it's decided 120 years after his death to name a pub after him. At the time of his death in 1635 (he said he was born in 1483) Thomas Parr was the talk of London and a household name having, so it's said, died age 152.

1756

The New Road (Pentonville Road) is built to link Battle Bridge (King's Cross) with The Angel.

1760

City Road is built to link the City with the Angel.

1761

(i) The mediaeval Moor Gate which released city dwellers from the smells of London into the fresh air of Islington is demolished and the stones used to repair London Bridge.

(ii) Oliver Goldsmith and his publisher John Newbery move into Canonbury Tower. Goldsmith stays two years, Newbury, five (until he dies).

1763

John Wilkes calls the King a liar. They will be bitter opponents in the public eye for the next fifteen years. The row will keep Wilkes out of parliament for eleven. 'Wilkes and Liberty' is graffiti'd all over London.

1770

John Dawes, property developer, starts building on Highbury Fields. He also demolishes the south wing of Tudor Canonbury Tower.

1772

Revd. George Strahan is vicar of St. Mary's. His sermons are so boring that churchgoers take a pack of playing cards with them. His friend Dr Johnson can often be seen shuffling down Upper Street to help Strahan pep them up.

1773

Built on a grid, Penton Ville is London's first planned suburb. Henry Penton MP for Winchester, Lord of the Admiralty, builds Penton Ville on 134 acres of open countryside each side of The New Road.

He's ordered to set the houses fifty foot back from the road so they have very long front gardens (a few survive near the Angel).

1776

Camden Passage is built.

1777

(i) George Dance the Younger designs Wesley's Chapel on City Road. He's instructed to build it well back from the road and hide it with trees so as not to offend C of E goers. He's also designing Finsbury Square.

(ii) The Countess of Huntingdon opens Spa Fields Chapel in Baynes Row (Exmouth Street) and starts her long battle with Rev. Sellon of St James Clerkenwell who tries to get it closed.

1780

The Gordon 'No Popery' Riots. Everything with a Roman Catholic connection is destroyed. Mr Hyde JP of 27 (now 61) Cross Street, orders out the militia. His house is ransacked and his possessions burnt in the street. The Artillery Company defends the Bank of England.

1782

(i) A new Sessions House is built on Clerkenwell Green. The crime rate is rising due to rapidly increasing population so new laws are introduced. 220 offences including pick pocketing and theft earn the death penalty. Execution and deportation are common.

(ii) Robert Pollard, printmaker, moves to 15 Baynes Row (Exmouth Street).

(iii) Joey Grimaldi, father of English clowns, makes his first stage appearance at Sadler's Wells age two.

1784

(i) Mary Wollstonecraft, arguably Britain's first feminist, opens a school initially on Upper Street but moves to much larger premises on Newington Green.

(ii) Britain's first hot air balloon takes off from Armoury House City Road.

(iii) Thomas Lord, cricket's first official groundsman, rents land at White Conduit House and forms the White Conduit Cricket Club (WCCC).

(iv) Rev. Strahan of St.Mary's is called out to administer the last rites for his old friend Dr Johnson.

1788

(i) St James, Clerkenwell, the mediaeval nunnery church, is, not surprisingly, falling to bits. A new one is built reflecting the social strata of the day. Men on the ground floor, women in the first balcony, servants on the second and untouchables behind doors in the panelling.

(ii) Alexander Aubert of Highbury builds an observatory from where he can see shipping on the Thames as far away as Gravesend. He watches the transit of Venus with George III who visits him whenever there is something worth seeing.

1790

Thomas Paine books into the Angel Inn for four nights to pen *The Rights of Man: Part One*. In the event, it takes four months. He advocates free health treatment, free education, old age pensions, unemployment benefits, maternity benefits and child allowances. He is charged with treason.

1791

John Wesley has dinner with his friend, John Horton at 25 Highbury Place. He dies at home the next day.

1792

The London Corresponding Society (LCS) is launched in Clerkenwell to show solidarity with the French and American revolutions. Committee members are arrested for treason and sent to the Tower. The trial at the Sessions House Clerkenwell Green lasts eight days. The men are found not guilty and celebrate with a huge triumphal march.

1794

A prison is built in Mount Pleasant, Cold Bath Fields, the largest in the UK with 1800 prisoners and 125 staff. With iron spikes on the roof and walls, it's nicknamed the 'Steele' after the Paris Bastille.

1795

(i) Forty thousand gather in Copenhagen Fields to support the LCS thirsty for a revolution in England.

(ii) Mary Wollstonecraft, now a single mother, returns from Paris where she witnessed the French Revolution. She moves to Finsbury Circus and, abandoned by the father of her daughter, twice tries to commit suicide.

1796

(i) Colonel Aubert of Highbury, horrified by the growing republican movement forms two regiments, The Loyal Islington Volunteers, one of infantry, one of cavalry.

(ii) Mary Wollstonecraft moves to Cumming Street, Pentonville. While here she publishes a travel book and reprints *The Vindication of The Rights of Women*.

(iii) Charles Lamb moves to Little Chapel Street (Chapel Market) to be near his sister who is in a local asylum (possibly Northampton House, St John Street where City University now stands).

1797

Mary Wollstonecraft marries radical philosopher William Godwin. She dies a few days after giving birth to Mary who will one day write the novel *Frankenstein*.

1798

The government puts heavy tax on gold and silver and a massive import duty on watch and clock casings throwing seven thousand in Clerkenwell out of work. In the first eleven weeks of its opening, a local soup kitchen saves thousands from starvation.

1799

(i) The London Corresponding Society Committee members are put in prison without trial and the Society declared illegal.

(ii) Mary Lamb is discharged from Islington asylum into her brother Charles' care. She is twelve years older than him. Neither marry. Charles devotes his life to looking after her. His closest friend from school days the poet Samuel Taylor Coleridge visits them in Chapel Street.

(ii) A group of worshippers at St Mary's Upper Street find they are getting little spiritual sustenance from the staid and starchy services. they start holding their own in a derelict chapel in Highbury Grove.

1800

10,000 live in Islington. More than five times as many live in Finsbury (55,515). Britain gets its first clown when Joe Grimaldi plays Guzzle the Drinking Clown at Sadler's Wells wearing a multi-coloured Harlequin costume and red half moons on a painted white face.

1802

(i) Augustus Pugin, a local architect, marries Catherine Welby, a local beauty, in St Mary's, Upper Street (where they will be buried in a family vault). The Pugin's live here for twenty years.

(ii) William and Dorothy Wordsworth visit Mary and Charles Lamb in Little Chapel Street. The old friends visit Bartholomew Fair together. One day Wordsworth will write about in *The Prelude*.

1803

The poet, Robert Southey and publisher Clio Rickman visit their old friends, the Lamb's, in Little Chapel Street.

1805

John Saunders, distressed by the blinding conjunctivitis suffered by troops returning from the Napoleonic wars, founds The London Dispensary For Curing Diseases Of The Eye in Charterhouse Square, the first of its kind in the world.

1806

(i) John Stuart Mill is born to James, founder of London University and Harriet at 12 Rodney Terrace Pentonville (demolished 1957).

(ii) Gold is in short supply following the Napoleonic wars so Abraham Newland, of 38 Highbury Place, Chief Cashier, Bank of England asks the Privy Council for permission to introduce paper money (banknotes) into British Currency. Each has his name and signature, is numbered and traceable. The drovers are relieved (highwaymen don't mug for bank notes).

(iii) The chapel in Highbury Grove has become too small for all the disaffected C of E worshippers (Unionists) who first formed in 1799. Henry Le Roux builds them a small, pretty, Georgian chapel in Compton Terrace.

(iv) Jane Taylor, born and bred in Islington writes *The Star*.

>Twinkle, twinkle, little star,
>
>How I wonder what you are!
>
>Up above the world so high,
>
>Like a diamond in the sky

It was published in 1806 in *Rhymes for the Nursery* by Jane and her sister Ann. Loved by children all over the world, one day Nelson Mandela will sing it to children at his retirement party.

1807

(i) Thomas Hood (age nine) future poet moves to 50 Lower Street (Essex Road) with his parents and lives here twenty years.

(ii) Henry Le Roux starts building Canonbury Square.

(iii) John Stuart Mill moves with his family from Pentonville to Newington Green.

(iv) The Camden Head is built in Camden Passage.

1808

Isaac D'Israeli moves his family including little Benjamin from Canonbury to 9 Upper Street (renumbered 215). Benjamin attends Dame Roper's Academy in Colebrooke Row. One day he will make it to Prime Minister.

1810

Robert Pollard and son James move from Exmouth Street to 11 Holloway Place where they open a successful print business.

1811

The Castle, Cowcross Street, is granted a pawnbroker licence (the only pub in the UK to hold one) when the Prince Regent, gambling in Turnmill Street, borrows money from the landlord and leaves his watch as surety.

1812

(i) When the tunnel through Highgate Hill collapses, John Nash builds a bridge to take traffic across the gap, a large arch supported by four small ones. This becomes Arch Way Road.

(ii) A road is carved through Le Roux' Canonbury Square blighting properties before they're sold.

(iii)The Regent's Canal is started, the last link in the Grand Union Canal from the north to the Thames.

(iv) Edward Lear is born at Bowman's Lodge Holloway Road where he lives until his father chucks him out at 16.

(v) Charles Lamb visits his friend Leigh Hunt in Coldbath Prison detained awaiting trial for calling The Prince Regent a fat, fifty year old Adonis.

1814

Percy Bysshe Shelley, baronet, poet, expelled from Oxford for publishing a book expounding atheism, a married man, elopes with sixteen year old Mary Wollstonecraft Godwin. Her step-sister Claire Clairmont goes with them and has a daughter by Lord Byron.

1815

The Artillery Company fight in Duke of Wellington's Battle of Waterloo.

1816

(i) Mary Godwin's half-sister Fanny Wollstonecraft commits suicide. A furious William Godwin refuses to identify her body so she's given a pauper's grave. Shelley's wife Harriet also commits suicide by drowning in the Serpentine.

(ii) Spa Fields Riot. The Militia is ordered to shoot to kill.

1818

(i) Despite a growing population, there's only one established church in Islington (St.Mary's Upper Street) so an Act of Parliament is passed to build Chapels of Ease (ment) in populous districts. After a thousand years Islington gets a second C of E, St Mary Magdalene is built in Holloway Road.

(ii) George Cruickshank, famous cartoonist moves to Claremont Square with his mother, brother Isaac and sister Eliza. He lives in Islington from the age of twenty-six to fifty-eight.

1819

James Hook (RA) is born in Northampton Square. Renowned for his English coastlines, 'The Samphire Gatherer' is in the Tate.

1820

(i) John Junius Booth, actor, off shoot of old Clerkenwell families the Booth's and Wilkes' (gin distillers) emigrates to America. Oh dear. There he will have a son, call him after the infamous John Wilkes, who will assassinate President Lincoln.

(ii) The Islington stretch of the Regent's Canal opens.

(iii) Opposing teams (Gown Boys v Scholars) of Charterhouse schoolboys start playing cloister football. Soccer hooligans are born.

1821

A Free Dispensary is opened in St Mary's Path, Upper Street. (rebuilt 1886) with two doctors, two surgeons and resident pharmacist. 31,571 patients are treated in the first twelve years. 28,620 are cured, 1318 relieved, 93 discharged, 124 transferred to hospital and 741 died. 675 are undergoing treatment. Closed 1948 (NHS).

1823

Population of Finsbury, 86,000, Islington, 22,000. Charles Lamb moves to Colebrooke Cottage, Colebrooke Row and stays till he retires. Famous friends who visit him here include Hazlitt, Wordsworth, Thomas Hood, Thomas Carlyle, Harrison Ainsworth, John Clare and Thomas de Quincey the opium eater.

1824

Cruickshank moves to 22 Myddellton Terrace (69 Amwell Street). He lived at 69 and next door at 71 when they were 22 and 23 Myddelton Terrace. He lives here twenty-five years

1825

Cruickshank and his cronies meet at Walter Ralegh's old house, now a pub, The Pied Bull, Upper Street to drink a toast to 'the immortal memory of Walter Raleigh'.

1826

(i) Charles Barry builds Holy Trinity Church, Cloudesley Square, St Peter's, Devonia Road, St. John's, Pemberton Gardens and St. Paul's, Hopping Lane (re-named St Paul's Road).

(ii) George Shillibeer offers the first, time-tabled (horse-drawn) bus service and is given the first bus franchise.

1830

(i) No.43 bus is launched. Battle Bridge is re-named King's Cross when a statue of George IV is put up at the cross-roads.

(ii) George Betjeman, great grandfather of the poet laureate, opens a cabinet making business near the Angel.

1831

(i) Every Sunday Michael Faraday famous inventor is seen walking to or from the Barnsbury Sandemanian Church where he is an Elder and gives sermons. He smiles to himself when he sees passers by run around the corner to come back and have a second look at him.

(ii) Shops are packed till midnight every night seven days a week. Rev Daniel Wilson of St Marys, Upper Street, founds The Lords Day Observance Society.

(iii) A licence is issued to convert a private house, 43 Hedge Row (45 Upper Street) into The Star and Garter public house. In 1976 after 142 years the historic name was changed to The Champion in 1983, The Passage then The Steam Passage.

1832

(i) Clerkenwell Rookeries are the worst in London. Thousands pour in looking for work living ten to a room. Hygiene is unknown, there's no running water, sanitation or sewerage. Clerkenwell's sweet tasting springs are long gone. Instead, the parish receives drainage from Hampstead and Highgate cemeteries and cess pits. Cholera is rife as is typhoid and small pox. No local government means no one takes responsibility. City Corporation buys ten acres in Holloway for a burial ground.

(ii) The Literary and Science Institute opens in Almeida Street.

(iii) Edwin, son of John Junius Booth is born in Baltimore. He becomes America's leading Shakespearean tragedian but is better known as the man whose brother assassinates Abraham Lincoln.

1833

For some reason George Cruickshank and his wife Mary move next door to No.23 (71 Amwell Street), his third and last address in Islington. He launches *The Comic Almanac* which he will produce from here for the next nineteen years. Twenty thousand buy the first issue.

1834

120,000 trade unionists gather on Copenhagen Fields to support the Tolpuddle Martyrs who were transported to Australia for starting a trade union. Local MP Dr Tom Wakley (founder of The Lancet) gets them a free pardon.

1836

(i) Robert Seymour, who has lived in Islington since he left school, shoots himself in the garden of his home 16 Park Place West (Liverpool Road). He had just returned from a meeting with Charles Dickens who criticised his illustrations for *The Pickwick Papers*.

(ii) Guiseppe Mazzini, republican, hounded out of Italy and France arrives in Little Italy Clerkenwell where he stays thirty for years.

1837

Charles Dickens is house hunting in Pentonville, London's most fashionable area which he knows well through his illustrators Robert Seymour and George Cruickshank. Prices are beyond his means so he buys in cheaper Bloomsbury where he writes *Oliver Twist*, the story of a slum boy living a few streets away in Saffron Hill Clerkenwell. The novel will make his name and that of Clerkenwell internationally famous.

1839

In America, Junius Brutus Booth has a third son (his first is John Junius, his second is Edwin). He calls him John Wilkes Booth.

1840

(i) Spa Fields Cemetery scandal. The graveyard meant to hold 1361 of our dearly departed holds 80,000.

(ii) Scandal alert. Prince George, cousin of (and once selected as the most suitable husband for) prim Queen Victoria marries Louisa Fair brother, 31, actress, mother of his three sons in St John's Church Clerkenwell. She goes by the name of Mrs Fitzgerald. Louisa, at 16, also has two sons by Charles Sutton, grandson of the Archbishop of Canterbury.

1841

The children of Field Lane Saffron Hill Clerkenwell stink to high heaven so are barred from school. A Ragged School is set up in Caroline Court. Forty-five boys and girls sit on the floor of one room and teachers wear hats to protect them from fruit and vegetables thrown at them through broken windows by hostile locals. Charles Dickens is the school's patron until he dies.

1842

The New Model Prison later called Pentonville Prison opens in Barnsbury but it's Pentonville not Barnsbury which becomes blighted. The portcullis gateway is designed by Sir Charles Barry. The rule of silence means that prisoners are not allowed to communicate with each other and have to wear masks while sitting in separate box pews in chapel. Those who don't go mad or commit suicide communicate by tapping on plumbing pipes.

1844

Shakespeare's plays disappeared when Cromwell closed the theatres in the 1640s. Sam Phelps of Canonbury Square revives them at Sadler's Wells.

1845

Joseph Chamberlain, aged 9 and his family moves to 25 Highbury Place (one son will be MP for Finsbury, another, Neville, will be PM). He's enrolled at a prep school in Canonbury Square.

1846

Caroline Chisholm, home from Australia, where she's a legend, moves to 3 Charlton Crescent where she establishes The Family Colonisation Loan Society. A close friend of Charles Dickens, she ends up on the Oz $5 note and Charles ends up on our £10.

1848

William Elgar piano tuner marries Anne Greening (parents of Sir Edward) in St Mary's Church in Upper Street

1849

Bones of martyrs from Tudor days are found outside Barts.

1851

(i) Kate Greenaway, aged 5, (illustrator) moves to Upper Street.

(ii) George (*Trilby*) Du Maurier, chemistry student at London University, moves to 44 Wharton Street and stays five years.

1852

(i) Yet another prison. Holloway, a House of Detention for 288 men 56 women and 56 juveniles opens for business complete with towers and turrets. Called The City Prison because it's built on an old cemetery owned by the city. J. B. Bunning, City architect, designs a copy of Warwick Castle. Among infamous guests detained at Her Majesty's Pleasure are Oscar Wilde, Emily Pankhurst, Sir Oswald and Lady Mosley, Ruth Ellis and Rosemary West.

(ii) The seven 500 year old elm trees in Seven Sisters Road are chopped down and seven new ones planted by the seven McRae sisters of Tottenham.

1854

(i) Fred Lillywhite non-pareil bowler professional cricketer (Lord's since 1827) for the MCC dies at his home and cricket shop at 10 Princes Terrace Caledonian Road.

(ii) Harriet Beecher Stowe author of *Uncle Tom's Cabin*, campaigner against slavery gives a lecture at Spa Fields Chapel Exmouth Street.

1855

Ellen Ternan, future mistress of Charles Dickens, moves into Park Cottage, St. Paul's Place with her mother and two sisters, actresses in Sam Phelps Shakespeare Company at Sadler's Wells.

1856

(i) The New River is filled in.

(ii) Islington: Home of Football. Pupa football, fostered at Charterhouse, flowers into the Football Association (FA) using (unwritten) rules of charging and offside football. Charterhouse v Westminster. Goal keeper is the only member of the eleven to whom a post is assigned, the other ten simply try to get control of the ball and keep it. Within three years terms such as forward, wing, and centre back are introduced. Handling the ball is allowed otherwise the game is much as it is now.

1857

(i) Dickens, rich and successful is experiencing a mid-life crisis. He's in love with Ellen Ternan of Islington, almost thirty years his junior. She's 18; he's 44, married with ten children. A frequent visitor to Park Cottage, Dickens hates the object of his affections living there saying the house is 'unwholesome and unhealthy' hot in summer and cold in winter, uncomfortable with cramped quarters. Smitten Dickens orders a bracelet to be sent to Park Cottage to Ellen but it's delivered in error to his wife Catherine who is devastated. Dickens, embarrassed to be rumbled toughs it out. He denies a romantic interest, feigns fury, and orders Catherine make amends by calling on the Ternan's to take tea at Park Cottage. Dickens leaves Catherine. His illustrator, George Cruickshank, 65, also takes a mistress. Childless George fathers ten children. His marriage is a happy one and his wife knows about his parallel life.

(ii) Finsbury Barracks City Road is rebuilt. Jennings builds the New Artillery Ground Militia Barracks in castellated style with battlements and turrets.

(iii) Australia refuses to take any more criminals so transportation is abolished.

1859

The Unionists now number seven hundred. Their tiny 1806 Union Chapel in Compton Terrace is bursting its seams.

1860

(i) Nine hundred slum homes in Clerkenwell are bulldozed to make way for the world's first underground railway. No compensation, no argument, no re-housing. 12,000 are on the streets left to fend for themselves resulting in 1104 child deaths An emergency soup kitchen opens and feeds 8,500 starving people in the first ten days. Between 1859 and 1867 38,000 displaced by the railways are kept alive by one soup kitchen alone. Another at Church Cottage, St Mary's Path will stay open until 1912.

(ii) Mrs Tealby opens Holloway Dogs Home. When she dies ten years later, it moves to Battersea.

(iii) Queen Victoria grants permission for the Artillery Company to use the prefix Honourable.

1861

(i) Following slum clearance to build the world's first underground railway, the population of Clerkenwell, for the first time, is lower than Islington (129,073 compared with 155,341).

(ii) Collins Music Hall opens on Islington Green.

(iii) Upper Street is called The Golden Mile. The Philharmonic, Empire, Deacons, Collins and thirty-two public houses have entertainment licenses.

(iv) Carlo Gatti of Little Italy sells ice from wells underneath the Regents Canal at Battle Bridge, King's Cross. Tons of ice take six days from Norway to reach him via Limehouse Docks. Today his warehouse is The London Canal Museum.

1862

Smithfield traders build The Agricultural Hall for The Smithfield Show. One entrance is on Upper Street, another is at the rear, Back Road (Liverpool Road).

1863

The world's first 'tube' train opens at Farringdon (*Punch* dubs it The Sewer Railway). Carriages are open trucks which 30,000 board on the first day.

1864

(i) Garibaldi visits Mazzini in Clerkenwell.

(ii) Shakespeare's First Folios turn up in Canonbury Square.

1865

(i) Fords Theatre Washington. John Wilkes Booth a disaffected confederate shoots President Lincoln. Wilkes Booth is tried and executed. The career of his brother Edwin Booth America's most illustrious actor of his era was not blighted. There is a portrait of him by John Singer Sargent in The Players Club Gramercy Park New York.

(ii) Walter Sickert, 5, is in Islington for an operation. He spends much of his long life here.

(iii) The King's Head is re-built in Upper Street

1866

Islington: Home of Care in the Community. Watercress girls, starving, crippled, ragged and dirty, forage for food. Many are blind. They pick through the flowers and watercress discarded by Farringdon Market stall holders and limp into tourist areas such as Covent Garden to resell them. Young John Groom of Sekforde Street, just 21, opens a centre where hot food is provided every day at noon for flower girls in the area. London is Europe's wealthiest capital but these girls have no fire, food or furniture in their slum dwellings. There is no drainage or clean water but plenty of disease, crime, drunkenness and prostitution. Before long he has a soup kitchen, clothing club, evening school and a Penny Bank. He founds The Watercress and Flower Girls Mission to train the girls to get them off the streets and into domestic service where at least they will have a home.

1867

The first ever Fenian (IRA) bomb explodes in Clerkenwell. They go on bombing for a hundred and thirty years. The blast demolishes Corporation Lane. Bowling Green Lane, Coburg St, Plumber Place, Rosoman St, St James Buildings, Seckforde St, Shorts Building and Woodbridge Street all suffer from reverberations. 40 of the 120 injured suffer permanent disabilities and fifteen people including a little girl die. A plaque on Kingsway College wall commemorates the tragedy, another inside St James Church Clerkenwell, was unveiled by Disraeli.

1870

Champagne Charlie, (George Leybourne) Islington's very own Oliver Reed and Britain's first pop singer dies at 42 of, well, champagne. For the sake of his art he is prevailed upon to advertise Moet and Chandon by working his way through their list of champagnes. At the end of each act he is almost comatose. At the end of the final act (life) he is semi-comatose all the time.

1872

Clerkenwell is a slum, a no go area, somewhere families do not want their sons to live so Charterhouse School relocates to Godalming, Surrey. A Merchant Tailor's School is built on the site. Speakers Corner also relocates from Clerkenwell Green to Hyde Park.

1873

French poets Verlaine and Rimbaud are living in King's Cross.

1876

Dr. Robert Bridges, old Etonian, future poet laureate, leaves Barts and reports for duty at the Great Northern Central Hospital, Caledonian Road (Caledonian Road Baths). In 1879 it and he move to Holloway Road. In 1885 (some sources say 1881) he leaves medicine to become a poet.

1877

(i) Union Chapel opens in Compton Terrace. An organist here writes *Once in Royal David's City*.

(ii) St. John Ambulance is founded at St. John's Gate

(iii) The world's first Grand Military Tournament is on at 'the Aggie' in Upper Street.

1879

(i) George Gissing, novelist friend of H. G. Wells, moves to Noel Road.

(ii) Sherlock Holmes meets Dr Watson at Barts Hospital.

1880

(i) The Angel Inn is rebuilt (present building). As a nod to the past it sports an 'Angel' frieze (still there).

(ii) The Grand Military Tournament patronised by royalty is now The Royal Tournament. It's held at The Agricultural Hall annually until 1906.

1883

(i) St Peter's RC Church, Little Italy holds a public procession, the first Holy Communion parade, since Elizabeth I made the practising of Catholicism illegal.

(ii) John Betjeman's grandfather moves to 13 Compton Terrace and stays fifteen years.

1884

San Francisco comes to Archway. A cable car is in use for thirty years (until 1910) when Highgate Tube opens.

1885

A measly twenty-five acres are all that's left of the three hundred acres that were once Highbury Fields. The Metropolitan Board of Works and Islington Vestry buy them for the public.

1886

(i) The Post Office take over the old prison at Mount Pleasant.

(ii) Seven new elm trees are planted in Seven Sisters Road by the seven Hibbert sisters, daughters of a butcher in High Road Tottenham.

1887

Sunday 13 November, George Bernard Shaw, William Morris and Annie Besant assemble on Clerkenwell Green to lead thousands singing La Marseillaise demanding the right to demonstrate. 15,000 constables cordon off Trafalgar Square, 3000 around Nelson's column. 100 strong cavalry, with bayonets fixed, are in front of The Grand Hotel. Mounted police carry long batons. 2500 Reserves protect Charing Cross and 100 Hyde Park. The Grenadier and Life Guards are on standby. 200 protesters end up in hospital and some die.

1888

(i) The ancient Order of St. John is re-instated.

(ii) Aubrey Beardsley (16) starts work in Wilmington Square.

(iii) The Church of The Holy Redeemer is built in Exmouth Market. Architect John Snedding had been itching to have a go at Renaissance and Henry Wilson, who took over when Snedding died, wanted to get away from 'conventional cheap Gothic'. Inside are two organs donated by Prince Albert from the Royal Chapel Windsor.

(iv) The ancient County of Middlesex is abolished. London, the largest single metropolis the world has ever seen, is so big it's created a County in its own right. The London County Council (LCC) is founded to take over the duties of the Metropolitan Board of Works. The London Government Act is passed. Islington is represented by four members in the political constituencies of Central and East Finsbury.

1889

The 800 seater Deacons Music Hall, Spa Green, St John's Terrace, Myddelton Place, Garnault Place, John Street, Cold Bath Square and bits of Mount Pleasant are all razed to make way for Rosebery Avenue to link Finsbury with Holborn. Named after Lord Rosebery, Liberal MP and first LCC chairman, it bridges the steep Fleet valley. Built in three sections, when the first is opened traffic is diverted from Exmouth Street which is pedestrianised. When costermongers move in to trade, shopkeepers complain but stall holders successfully apply to the Vestry for licences. They are still there.

1890

Islington: Home of the May Day March. 4 May. The World's First May Day March starts from Clerkenwell Green with members of twenty-eight local radical associations demanding an eight hour working day.

1891

Charles Cruft of Holloway Road launches Crufts Dog Show at 'the Aggie'.

1892

(i) The people of Finsbury elect Dadabhar Naoroji, Liberal MP, Britain's first non-white to The House of Commons to the horror of Lord Salisbury who said a black man was unelectable. Naoroji, dubbed Narrow Majority, Professor of Mathematics, arrived in Clerkenwell from India in 1855 determined to become an MP and fight British Rule in India. Naoroji is a mentor to Mahatma Ghandi when they meet on the Indian National Congress. He returned home in 1906 and died there eleven years later. He will have to wait until 1993 until his astonishing achievement is officially commemorated when a plaque goes up on Finsbury Town Hall unveiled by Diane Abbott MP, Chris Smith MP and Sir David Steele.

(ii) Local residents, the Grossmith brothers, make Holloway famous in *Diary Of A Nobody*.

(iii) Michael Stephens of Henry Stephens & Co Ink Manufacturers (est 1832) builds a factory in Gillespie Road. It resembles a Venetian palazzo and has an illuminated chimney.

(iv) William Britains opens his Toy Soldier Factory in Hornsey Rise to sculpt and perfect hollow cast lead soldiers. He makes sets of life guards, five in a box, price one shilling. He follows with all the British Regiments in full dress uniform, Imperial Yeomanry, Boer War Cavalry and infantry with spring loaded guns.

1895

Oscar Wilde is in Holloway Prison Parkhurst Road for two months on remand awaiting trial. He brought an action for criminal libel against the Marquess of Queensbury and lost. He was then charged with offences under the Criminal Law Amendment Act. He is visited by Bosie (Lord Alfred Douglas) every day. After the trial he's taken to Pentonville Prison in Caledonian Road to begin two years hard labour before transferring to Wandsworth then Reading Gaol.

1896

(i) Britain's first public film show is at Collins Music Hall, Islington Green. Also on the bill is George Robey and Dan Leno.

(ii) Technical education is in demand. Land is given by earl of Northampton to found Northampton Institute in St John's Road. The City churches no longer have parishioners so the City Parochial Fund donates mega bucks. The Livery Companies are by now little more than elitist gentleman's clubs with more money than they know what to do with so direct some of their excess funds into education. Big commercially led businesses in the City need an educated workforce so also contribute. The government makes up the shortfall. Only technical subjects are offered. Designed by E. W. Mountford architect of The Old Bailey.

1897

Rev. Barlow of St Mary's, asks his brother to design him a new vicarage. His brother is the architect William Barlow who built St. Pancras Station.

1898

The Motor Show is at the 'Aggie'

1899

Moorfield's Eye Hospital opens in City Road, once part of the old moor fields.

1900

(i) St Mary's Hall in the old Aggie, the first proper cinema in Britain, opened with a sixteen piece orchestra. Films shown are *Count Zeppelins Warship*, *A Visit to the Spiritualist* and *Rush Hour at the Angel*. A few months later it has a name change, Islington Empire Theatre. Islington is film mad. Even Northern Polytechnic Institute, Holloway Road is showing a film of the South African War (Boer War). At its peak, the borough will have forty cinemas which people go to two or three times a week.

(ii) The Trades Unions Congress (TUC) forms the Labour Party in the Congregational Memorial Hall, Farringdon Street. A hundred years later Tony Blair an Islingtonian, by sleight of hand, manages to sideline them from his New Labour Party.

(iii) John Nash's bridge spanning Archway Road is replaced with the present one by Sir Alexander Binnie, chief engineer LCC.

1901

(i) Population a staggering 436,701. Some women have thirty children. Houses are in multiple occupation. Each room has a coal fire which along with the railways cause pea souper smogs. For those in a job the minimum hours of work is 55 hours a week, thousands are on parish welfare, barefoot children scour rubbish bins for food. Medication is available only to those who can pay;

stories of cancer sufferers with no access to pain killers smashing their heads against the wall to alleviate suffering are common.

(ii) Nurse Edith ('patriotism is not enough') Cavell is Night Superintendent at the Whittington. She has just arrived from The London Hospital Stepney where she worked for five years. She stays throughout 1901 and 1902. Nurse Cavell was executed by the Germans in 1915 (WWI)

1902

Lenin. A Russian Marxist exile in London receives a letter from Munich asking him to approach Comrade Harry Quelch, editor of *Justice*, Twentieth Century Press, 37a Clerkenwell Green to see if he will print Lenin's *Iskra* (the spark). So it is that Clerkenwell becomes for over a year the headquarters of the Russian revolution. In Russia, trade unions and newspapers are prohibited; imprisonment is the punishment for belonging to a Socialist organisation so all radicals operate from abroad. Vladimir Ilyich Ulyanov Lenin. leader of the 1917 Russian Revolution, one of history's giants, destined to become the first democratic ruler of Russia and his wife Nadia rent rooms in 30 Holford Square to mastermind the most disruptive revolution in world history. He takes the pseudonym Jacob Richter. Out of the blue, a young (22) man knocks their door. His name is Lev Bronstein aka Trotsky. Just arrived from exile in Siberia, he tells Lenin that copies of *Iskra* delivered into Russia via Stockholm through Finland or via Brindisi on to Odessa are lost, seized or sent to the wrong addresses for redistribution. What's to be done? Lenin's 'spark' which lights the flame of revolution is smuggled into Russia wrapped around the legs of supporters inside their knee high leather boots. *Iskra* literally walks into Russia. Harry Quelch prints the underground newspaper on his flat bed machine, the text set by a Russian compositor in the East End. Seventeen issues, Nos. 22 to 38, are printed here between April 1902 and May 1903. Quelch partitions part of the printing works as Lenin's editorial base and finds a writing table, bookshelf and chair (now listed an historic monument). Tom Quelch, Harry's son, a compositor, remembers Lenin (a small stocky young man with as pointed ginger beard) being astonished that the Social Democratic Federation, a legal political party, prints a weekly paper no more sophisticated than *Iskra*.

1903

Lenin and comrades plan the third Russian Social Democratic Labour Party Congress in their favourite meeting place, the upstairs room of The Crown and Woolpack pub in St John Street. Usually the landlord is told it is a meeting for Trades Unionists, this time the room is booked for The Foreign Barbers of London Association. DI Fitch of Scotland Yard hides in the cupboard to overhear the meeting but couldn't report back because in Russian. Another time at The Old Red Lion, DI Fitch disguises himself as a waiter and gets hold of the Minutes and Agenda but when the police arrive to make enquiries Lenin escapes in a food shaft (dumb waiter). The purpose of the meeting is the same, to overthrow the Tsar. Lenin heads the Bolsheviks opposed by Trotsky (nine years younger) who leads the Mensheviks. Lenin's policy stipulates only active revolutionaries willing to do anything to establish Communism. Trotsky, a Menshevik (minority) is a moderate who wants to admit anyone sympathetic to the cause. Lenin wins. The history of Russia might have been different had Trotsky prevailed. Brussels is decided upon as the most central venue for the Third Congress. However, Belgium refuses entry so the Congress is held in London.

1904

(i) Charles Hill is born in York Road. Age two the family moves to Liverpool Buildings, Highbury Station Road. He is The Radio Doctor during WW2, MP for Luton (1950-1963) Minister of Housing (1961) Chairman ITA (1963-67) Lord Hill (1963) Chairman BBC (1967-1972).

(ii) Keir Hardie MP Merthyr Tydfil founder of Independent Labour Party (ILP) HQ Drayton Park, and Ramsay MacDonald, first Labour PM address a mass meeting at Highbury Corner followed later in the year by another mass meeting of the unemployed at Grand Theatre Islington High Street.

1905

(i) Duke of Fife unveils Sir Bertram McKennal's figure of 'Glory', the South African War Memorial Highbury Fields erected to commemorate 110 local men (including many from HAC) killed in the Boer War. The Australian sculptor designed George V coinage, memorial tomb of Edward VII, St. George's Chapel Windsor, the National Memorial Waterloo Place, public memorial to Thomas Gainsborough in Sudbury and the statue of George Nathaniel, Foreign Secretary outside 1 Carlton House Terrace Carlton Gardens.

(ii) The No.19 bus route is launched.

1907

The Lenin's are back in Finsbury (16 Percy Circus) for the Fifth Congress of Russian Social Democrat Labour Party prohibited by Denmark, Sweden and Norway. The Brotherhood Church (more a meeting hall than chapel) Southgate Road is the venue (invited by left wing Reverend Swann who works for *The Daily Herald*). The

Congress is attended by a record number (336) of Russian revolutionary delegates including Lenin, Josef Stalin, Maxim Gorky, a hundred and five Bolsheviks, ninety seven Mensheviks, reporters, photographers and twelve detectives. Lenin can't pay the delegates fares back home so Party members take the hat round Russians domiciled in London. One benefactor, after hearing the speeches in the Brotherhood Church, lends Lenin £1700. The money is returned with interest ten years later. The Brotherhood Church, paradoxically, is famous later for pacifist meetings attended by Bertrand Russell.

1908

(i) Emmeline Pankhurst and other Suffragettes on hunger strike in Holloway Prison are force fed by having a rubber tube pushed down the throat or up the nostril. She launched The Women's Social and Political Union a feminist movement with her daughter Christabel to campaign for votes for women.

(ii) Fenner Brockway, conscientious objector, Labour candidate for Finsbury Council moves into The Claremont Square Mission then into 60 Myddelton Square (blue plaque unveiled by himself in 1975) home of Secretary of the Independent Labour Party. Half a dozen or so socialists live here as a community.

Brockway, committed pacifist will found CND in 1954 and be the Labour Party's first peer in 1964.

1910

Americans, Harvey and Cora Crippen, of Hilldrop Crescent Holloway don't get on. He poisons her, chops her up, wraps her remains in his pyjamas bought from Jones Bros Holloway Road (now Waitrose) and throws her head in the sea. He's hanged at Pentonville.

1911

(i) Fred Seddon of Tollington Park poisons Eliza Barrow, his lodger. He's hanged at Pentonville.

(ii) The No.4 bus route is launched.

1912

(i) Charlie Chaplin and Stan Laurel work the Islington halls this year. Charlie makes one of his last appearances in Britain at Collins Music Hall Islington Green before emigrating to America.

(ii) John Groom's Watercress and Flower Girls Mission, Clerkenwell produce thirteen million cotton roses for the first Alexandra Rose Day. They raise £18k for hospital work.

1913

(i) *The New Statesman* is launched 14-16 Farringdon Lane as a mouthpiece for The Fabian Society and to support The Labour Party.

(ii) Arsenal FC (founded 1886 in Woolwich) comes to Highbury.

1914

(i) The Great War. Islington's German population (3000) is interned or deported (The Royal Family change their name from Saxe Gotha Coburg Battenburg to Windsor). Tunnelling at Mount Pleasant Post Office (for transportation of mail and parcels) is suspended. Tunnels so far excavated are used to store the Elgin Marbles and other priceless artefacts from the British Museum, Tate and National Portrait Gallery. Just before the war, Islington had twenty-nine cinemas, at the end, it has seventeen. People need news of the war. Cossors at Aberdeen Works, Highbury Grove can't churn out radios quickly enough to meet demand. Their 'Melody Maker' is a best seller.

(ii) George Smith drowns his 'wife' in her bath at Archway. He 'married' seven women and drowned three.

1919

Paramount Pictures convert an electricity sub-station into Islington Film Studios and employ Alfred Hitchcock as subtitler (films are silent). He stays twenty years.

1921

Dr. Marie Stopes opens Britain's first birth control clinic in Holloway.

1923

(i) Arnold Bennett writes *Riceyman Steps* about a miserly second hand bookseller in Clerkenwell.

(ii) Len Harvey, 16, future world light-heavyweight boxing champion moves to Caledonian Road.

1924

(i) Michael Balcon launches Gainsborough Films at Islington Film Studios.

(ii) The old Clerks Well is re-discovered in the cellar of *The New Statesman* offices in Farringdon Road.

1925

Walter Sickert paints 'The Hanging Gardens of Islington' from his studio 56 Noel Street (now Road) overlooking the Regent's Canal.

1927

The Post Office high speed underground railway between Paddington and Whitechapel is opened by George V and Queen Mary. The electric system is fully automatic and operates around the clock. At 35mph compared with 7mph over ground, mail from Liverpool Street to Paddington takes thirteen minutes. The railway is nicknamed the Ghost Train because it has no passengers, guards or drivers. Seventy feet below ground, twenty three miles long, the track, two foot wide in nine foot two way tunnels, runs every four minutes. Used solely for the movement of letters and parcels it carries mail for 22 out of 24 hours. Controlled automatically the carriages carry ten million bags of mail every year between six major sorting offices and two main line stations. The Sorting Office, half way along (this part of the tunnel is 6½ miles long) covers seven and a half acres, its three thousand workforce sends twenty million items of mail to twenty-two million addresses.

1928

(i) Evelyn Waugh, novelist, and his bride the Hon. Evelyn Gardner, niece of the earl of Caernarfon (who funded Howard Carter's excavation of Tutankhamen's tomb (1923) and died weeks later) move to Canonbury Square. He writes *A Handful of Dust* about his sorry year here.

(ii) Soap Box Soper (Rev. Donald, later Lord Soper) moves to Holloway.

1931

(i) Lilian Baylis buys Sadler's Wells from where she will found the Royal Ballet and English National Opera.

(ii) Walter Sickert opens an art school at 1, Highbury Place.

1932

Herbert Chapman Arsenal FC manager campaigning since 1925 at last persuades London Transport to change the name of the 1906 Gillespie Road tube station tube to Arsenal. The famous West Stand is built which in seventy years time causes problems for the club when it want to demolish it.

1933

The Nazi Party in Germany burns Karl Marx' books on the 50th anniversary of his death. The House on Clerkenwell Green is renamed The Marx Memorial Library to commemorate him.

1934

(i) Monopoly (the board game) makes Angel, Islington famous all over Britain. Famous as a near slum.

(ii) The new curate at St.Mary's is David Coggan; by 1974 he's Archbishop of Canterbury

1935

Michel Saint Denis one of the most influential men in theatre opens The London Theatre Studio in Providence Hall Upper Street. (behind Screen On The Green). Among others he trains Peter Ustinov, Marius Goring, Edith Evans, Michael Redgrave, Laurence Olivier and Alec Guinness. He cross fertilises English, French and American theatre, introduces theatre in the round and founds The National Theatre. He also appears briefly in Alfred Hitchcock's *Secret Agent.*

1936

(i) Peter Sellers is a day boy at St. Aloysius College, Hornsey.

(ii) Tudor Films (owned by the Marquis of Ely) are at Highbury Film Studios.

(iii) The Campaign for Abortion Law Reform opens in Islington High Street. It takes them thirty years to get abortion de-criminalised.

1937

The Ustinov's don't know what to do with young Peter, 16, so send him to Michel Saint Denis a friend who runs the drama school with George Devine in Upper Street. Mrs Ustinov paints scenes for the theatre run by the 'tweedy pipe smoker with yellow hair'.

1938

(i) War is in the air. Gainsborough Films reflect it in Alfred Hitchcock's classic *The Lady Vanishes* his ninety-seven minute passport to Hollywood. Orson Welles no mean Director himself saw it eleven times. En route back to England aboard The Orient Express from Switzerland an old lady disappears and two passengers (Michael Redgrave and Margaret Lockwood) look for her. Although the dumpy middle age lady in tweeds disappears from a train in Europe the whole film is shot in Poole Street, Islington. Hitch (like Woody Allen) isn't keen on going out on location but his meticulous attention to detail makes Poole Street a very credible Europe. Sydney Gilliat and Frank Launder suggested Gainsborough buy the rights to *The Wheel Spins* by Ethel Lina White and they adapt it for screen. Hitch says he can film it in a month (he did it in five weeks) His wife Alma and daughter Pat are on the set with him.

(ii) Gaumont British buys Gainsborough Pictures.

(iii) The Boulting Brothers *The Arsenal Stadium Mystery* features the 1938 line up.

(iv) Finsbury Borough Council introduces cradle-to-grave health care when it opens Pine Street Clinic designed by Berthold Lubetkin.

1939

Another World War. Old air raid sirens are tested, blackout curtains go up (any glimmer will guide enemy bombs) street lights and traffic lights are masked, torch beams stuck over with paper, smoking in the street is banned and the edges of pavements painted white to indicate the road. Out That Light posters go up everywhere. Sign posts, milestones, station names are removed and shop signs painted over if they show destinations (eg.The Islington Bakery). Ships bringing food to Britain are sunk by German submarines so goods are rationed. Everyone has a Ration Book and registers with one grocer for their allotted four ounces of butter, ham and bacon and twelve ounces of sugar a week and with one butcher for four ounces of meat. Food, soap, petrol, coal and clothes are all rationed. All boys still at school have to wear short trousers to save material. Rationing won't end until 1954. Non-Brits are viewed with paranoid suspicion so although many change their foreign names, are locked up or deported. Mussolini declares war on Britain, so Italians (here since the Middle Ages) are officially classified as enemy aliens and deported (MI5 says Clerkenwell cafés are run by fascist revolutionaries). St Aloysius College Hornsey

Lane relocates to Cambridgeshire for the duration so Peter Sellers' school days are over. People who moved to Clerkenwell to be near the city, now move out because it's too near. The densely populated area becomes commercial. Hitchcock goes to America. Many cinemas close and never re-open. Theatres are closed so Sadler's Wells Ballet and Opera go on tour (entertainers are exempt from call up to give concerts). Caledonian Road Market (the Cally) is closed and used to store armaments. Betjeman & Sons Pentonville Road (est.1820) closes. The Marquess of Northampton dismantles the Elizabethan Oak Room, Sir John Spencer Room and The Compton Room in Canonbury Tower and stores panelling and carvings at his home in Castle Ashby, Northamptonshire. The two hundred and fifty year old Oak Room in the Metropolitan Water Board Building Rosebery Avenue carved by Grinling Gibbons is dismantled and stored. Islington sponsors a Spitfire Mark V6 sent to Gibraltar to be used in training. Parts of Charterhouse are gutted by incendiaries (fire bombs) so pensioners are evacuated. A bomb hits gas and water mains under an air raid shelter in Goswell Road. 200 are blown to smithereens. A flying bomb hits the Gaumont, Holloway Road. Another lands on Mount Pleasant Sorting Office so it moves into the Aggie. 958 Islingtonians die and 78000 homes are war damaged. Camden Passage is a bomb site, St Mary's, Upper Street and St John's, St John Square are burned out. Islington is bombarded with German VIs and V2s small jet propelled pilot less aircraft called flying or buzz bombs.

Eight thousand VIs are launched on Britain from occupied France and Holland. Thirteen thousand of the world's first ballistic missile, a German V2 bomb are launched. One of five hundred and seventeen which land on London falls on Highbury Corner, one of the last to be launched, turning the corner into a roundabout. The wonderful St Pancras look-alike station at Highbury Corner is demolished as are the last five (some sources say 22) houses in Compton Terrace. Twenty-four are killed and one hundred and fifty-five seriously injured. Poor old Islington, progressively unlovely since the 1800s, worse after the railways carved it up, battered by World War One, after a second devastating war is a deeply depressing slum and many can't wait to get out.

1940

Highbury Neighbourhood Watch telephones Scotland Yard to report that German paratroopers and uniformed Nazis have captured Highbury Film Studios. They're film extras.

1943

Fascists Oswald and wife Lady Diana (Mitford Guinness) Mosley are in Holloway Prison.

1944

George Orwell moves to Canonbury Square with wife Eileen and adopted son Richard. This is the last home Eileen or George have, six years later, both are dead. *Animal Farm* is published in 1945, Eileen dies in 1946, Orwell in 1950. Bits of *1984* are written here but the bulk is completed in the Orkneys.

1945

Rod Stewart is born at Archway where his parents own a newsagents. He will go to the same school as Ray and Dave Davies of The Kinks. Alan Parker, future famous film director, is born in Canonbury.

1946

Crowds gather outside Pentonville prison when Neville Heath, murderer, is hanged.

1947

(i) J. Arthur Rank buy Highbury Studios to groom promising young actors and actresses in his Rank Charm School for stardom. Groups of thirty attend for six months. Rank pays them £20 a week. The school which is here until 1952 teaches elocution, deportment and fencing. Graduates are Joan Collins, Christopher Lee, Diana Dors, Dirk Bogarde and Kay Kendall. Michael Caine, 17, is turned down when he's caught smoking in the loo.

(ii) Poet Louis MacNeice moves to Canonbury Park South.

1949

Angus McBean, Islington photographer 'discovers' Audrey Hepburn.

1950

Thousands gather outside Pentonville prison the day Timothy Evans is hanged (for two murders he didn't commit).

1952

The Tavistock Repertory Company moves to Canonbury Tower.

1953

ATV take over Highbury Studios to film Sunday Night Theatre, Emergency Ward Ten, Take Your Pick and Double Your Money.

1954

(i) Fenner Brockway who lived in Myddelton Square founds CND (HQ Holloway Road) to campaign against nuclear weapons. Thousands carry its famous logo when Monsignor Bruce Kent (priest at St John's, Duncan Terrace) and Bertrand Russell lead them from Trafalgar

Square to Aldermaston, Berkshire. When seven thousand link arms around nuclear weapon centres, sarcastic Defence Secretary Michael Heseltine dismisses them as 'naive'.

(ii) The Clean Air Act is passed.

1955

(i) Thousands gather outside Holloway prison as Ruth Ellis is hanged for murdering lover David Blakely.

(ii) The Bloomsbury Group live in squares and love in triangles. Vanessa Bell and Duncan Grant leading lights of the movement live at 26 Canonbury Square. Grant, once her brother's lover, is 70 and Vanessa 76. The couple knew Picasso and Matisse and helped organise the first exhibition of Impressionist paintings in London.

1956

The People's Picture Palace, Holloway Road becomes The National Youth Theatre (NYT) of Great Britain. It will spawn Daniel Day Lewis, Helen Mirren, Timothy Dalton, Ian McShane et al.

1957

(i) John Osborne takes Vivien Leigh and Laurence Olivier to Collins Music Hall, inspiration for *The Entertainer* written specifically for Olivier. Osborne said 'Collins Music Hall in Islington was about to be swept away. Bulldozers and iron balls were poised. I was especially keen that we should go a few times to Collins where I had witnessed some of the very worst acts imaginable'. By the time the film is released Vivien Leigh is history, Olivier married Joan Plowright his co-star on the film. *The Entertainer* is about a mediocre small time music hall comedian Archie Rice who perseveres with corny end of pier patter to an audience which has only come in for the strip tease.

(ii) Barbara Castle MP for Blackburn moves to John Spencer Square, St Paul's Road.

1958

The Tower Theatre put on a new play by unknown newcomer. Harold Pinter's *The Birthday Party* premièred at Lyric, savaged by theatre critics, slammed by theatre goers is withdrawn after three performances but Islington audiences love it. Pinter writes to the Tower: 'The Tavistock production...meant a great deal to me'.

1959

(i) John Lydon is born in Benwell Street, off Holloway Road. Eileen and John Lydon (both 18) change Britain forever via the first of their four sons. Pete Townshend says he's in awe of Lydon who 'changed the world'. Paul McCartney will ask to make a record with him (the idea horrifies John). He goes to the local Catholic school, Sir William of York (later amalgamated into St Aloysius College) Gifford Street off York Way near Pentonville Prison. His father works on the North Sea oil rigs. A hard life impoverished in everything except parental love, pride and affection. One passion of John's, Arsenal FC, will never diminish.

(ii) RADA actors Joe Orton and Kenneth Halliwell move into a Noel Road bedsit. The vendor tells them that Islington is up and coming and the local pub sells salad (The Slug and Lettuce has a huge salad bar). Like other ill fated Islingtonians (the Crippens, Fred Seddon and Eliza Barrow, George Smith and Margaret Lofty, the Orwell's and Joe Meek) Orton and Halliwell will not move out alive.

(iii) The media dubs Islington 'The New Chelsea' when local celebs help John Payton save Camden Passage. He has discovered that the Council plans to demolish it and build yet more council flats. His 'mole' at the Town Hall is young Paul Jones one of his customers at the music shop who goes on be lead singer with Manfred Mann. The Passage goes up market when it gets its first antique dealer; it now has the greatest concentration of antiques in Europe with 350 specialist dealers in 200 yards.

1960

(i) Council plans are afoot to demolish Bevan, Packington and Prebend Streets to build a concrete six storey block of flats for 1632 residents. Horrified residents form a Residents Association backed by The Islington Society and a long public enquiry follows. Worse, the GLC, to solve the traffic problem at the Angel is planning a three lane motorway to run alongside The Regent's Canal with underpasses and flyovers. Six years later there's one resident left in Arlington Avenue. Plans go through and the predicted socially disastrous Packington Estate completed 1970, by 1980 is a no go area run by street gangs.

(ii) Rod Stewart (16) of Archway leaves school. He doesn't fancy becoming an accountant like his brother so becomes a grave digger. In less than a decade (1970) *Gasoline Alley* will make him rich and famous.

(iii) The Angel Inn, here for over three hundred years, closes.

(iv) John Betjeman publishes autobiographical poem *Summoned By Bells* mentioning many places in the borough.

(v) Joe Meek another young gifted homosexual whose shares Orton's hobby of dicing with danger moves to Islington and he also will meet a violent tragic early end just months after Orton. Unlike Orton who makes it into the Dictionary of National Biography (DNB) Meek doesn't. Writing is considered worthy of merit, producing hit pop records is not. Joe Meek, a musical genius, Britain's first truly independent record from 304 Holloway Road competes with astonishing success against giants EMI, Decca, Pye, Parlophone, Columbia and HMV. Meek is so far ahead of his time no one can touch him. He produces unique outer space sounds on hit after hit record from two bedrooms used as recording studios. Besides the massive *Johnny Remember Me* some of his other hits from here are *Tell Laura I Love Her, Will You Love Me Tomorrow, I'll Walk the Line* and *Have I the Right* by the Honeycombs. Among the young hopefuls who beat a path to this door is Rod Stewart, 16, who lives just up the road at Archway and young Tommy Scott (Tom Jones). He and his group the Senators drive here from Wales. From here, he gives Chas'n Dave, Screaming Lord Sutch, Freddie Starr, Jonathan King and Davy Jones (Bowie) their first break.

1962

(i) *The Daily Mirror* headline 'Gorilla in The Roses' refers to a monkey's head stuck in the middle of a rose in Collins *Guide to Roses*. Joe Orton, aged 29, achieves fame when the newspaper reports on his and Halliwell's habit of stealing books from local libraries, altering the book jackets or rewriting the blurb inside the fly leaf. They appear at Clerkenwell Magistrates Court and found guilty of stealing 72 library books, defacing 44 dust covers (now in Islington Library archives) and removing 1653 colour plates from art books total damage £450.

(ii) From his bedroom recording studio in 304 Holloway Road comes Joe Meek's phenomenally successful *Telstar* a weird haunting tune written by him to commemorate Russia's Sputnik . It's in the Top 20 for over a year.

(iii) A young curate begins his ministry at St.Mary's. George Carey doesn't know it but destiny decrees he will be The Right Honourable, The Right Reverend Lord Archbishop of Canterbury. He will live in Lambeth Palace, take his seat in the House of Lords, and be jostled in his own pulpit at Canterbury Cathedral by Gay Rights activists. Oh yes. He will also become a dedicated Arsenal fan and set the C of E on its heels when he insists on the ordination of women priests.

(iv) Robert Carrier of Barnsbury Square gives slummy Islington a new trendy image when he opens a restaurant in bombed out Camden Passage, goes on TV with *Carrier's Kitchen*, writes and sells two million copies of *Great Dishes of the World* and cooks a birthday dinner for the Queen Mother (which she said was the best meal eaten in her life)

1963

A Labour politician living in Islington long before Tony Blair brings down the Tory government. Barbara Castle MP invites fellow MPs Richard Grossman, Harold Wilson and George Wigg to dinner in her flat and tells them she intends to raise 'the Profumo affair' in the House. They agree to back her. Her question 'Was it true that the Minister of War was involved?' brings Profumo to the dispatch box to say there has been 'no impropriety whatsoever 'in his relationship with Christine Keeler.

1964

Barbara Castle MP is Minister for Overseas Development.

1965

(i) London Local Government Act. Counties of London and Middlesex now Greater London Council (GLC) The ancient borough of Finsbury (St Luke's, St James,

Bunhill, Pentonville, Clerkenwell) to its horror is absorbed into the Borough of Islington. (Finsbury Circus is now in the City, Finsbury Park in Haringey, Pentonville Prison, not in Pentonville but Barnsbury, Holloway Prison is in Parkhurst Road (Parkhurst Prison is in the Isle of Wight) Camden Passage is not in Camden but in Islington. All very confusing). Letters Patent grant Islington a new Coat of Arms. Wavy blue lines symbolise water, arrows for archery. yellow crescent on red background Arms of Thomas Sutton, founder of Charterhouse School, yellow rings of Dick Whittington Coat of Arms, Maltese Cross Knights of St John, Book of Learning is Northampton Institute

(ii) Barbara Castle (who can't drive) is Minister of Transport. PM Wilson is desperate for an effective transport policy. She introduces seat belts and the breathalyser.

1966

(i) Benjamin Britten and Peter Pears who have worked with Sadler's Wells since Lilian Baylis took over in 1931, move to 99 Offord Road and stay four years before moving to 8 Halliford Street. Also in Offord Road in 1966 is another musical household name. Chris Farlowe and the Thunderbirds (born John Deighton in Offord Road 1940) get to number one with *Out of Time* written by Mick Jagger. His house is besieged by the music press and teenage fans. In the 1990s he opens an antiques shop in Canonbury Lane called Out of Time.

(ii) Labour government's Tony Crosland vows 'to destroy every f***ing grammar school in England, Wales and Northern Ireland' including Highbury Grove, St. Aloysius and Dame Alice Owen. Dr Rhodes Boyson a fully paid up member of the Labour Party, a Grammar School boy and strict disciplinarian is appointed Head, Highbury Grove School (the Grammar School, Barnsbury Sec. Mod. and Laycock Street School for 'problem boys' now Highbury Grove Comprehensive). Michael Duane headmaster of the failing Risinghill School is in the news for banning corporal punishment, the Press is camped outside the headmaster's door at the failing William Tyndale School, the White Lion Free School is run by the pupils who literally, do what they want which includes attending lessons and when Pink Floyd needs a group of children to sing on *We Don't Need No Education* (on The Wall) where do they go but to the failing Islington Green School. Dr Boyson makes many enemies in Labour run Islington Council criticising what he says are 'loony left permissive policies trying to inculcate a socialist revolution via the classroom' providing carte blanche for slack teaching methods, abolishing all rote learning (including multiplication tables) and expecting pupils to learn how to read by discovery. By 1971 on entrance to Highbury Grove many 11 year olds have the reading ability of an 8 year old. The school with its impressive academic results is besieged by parents who want their sons to go there but are ordered to enrol them at their nearest school so in Boyson's 'catchment' area property prices rise by 20%. In 1974 his school is beginning to resemble a worker's co-operative. Dr Boyson's worst fears over comprehensive education come true. He bows out of Highbury and out of the Labour Party to become Conservative MP for Brent North. He lost the battle but won the war. By 1999 Islington schools are so bad a Labour government hands them over to a private management consultancy.

1967

Kenneth Halliwell bludgeons Joe Orton to death then commits suicide.

1968

(i) Barbara Castle is at Windsor Castle with the Queen when Harold Wilson telephones asking her to be First Secretary of State and Secretary of State for Employment. She settles down in John Spencer Square to write her White Paper *In Place of Strife*. But there's more to life than white papers and she takes her mother to The Tower Theatre to see Aristophanes *Lysistrata*.

(ii) Anna Scher, drama teacher, turns around the lives of local kids. Without her they would never have thought of being on the telly, let alone a celeb. She takes over an empty chapel in 70 Barnsbury Road for an after school drama club and seventy children turn up. Among her first recruits are *Birds of a Feather* duo Linda Robson and Pauline Quirke. They are typical of the children from local Council estates, unaware that there is anything unusual in not having hot water in their flats or that they are seen as deprived or under-privileged. *Grange Hill* and *Eastenders* Susan Tully is another early recruit. 10% of drama club members 'go professional' (not a theatre school, the words 'Star' and 'Fame' are taboo) including Gillian Taylforth, Martin Kemp and Kathy Burke (when she returned from Cannes in 1998 clutching her award for *Nil By Mouth* the first person she went to see was Anna Scher).

1969

Dan Crawford buys The Kings Head and turns around the fortunes of poor old Upper Street half of which is still boarded up from war damage. He re-introduces a very old English concept, pub theatre, the first since Shakespeare's time. His theatre is the oldest fringe venue in Britain. By 1980 Islington has re-invented itself into off off Broadway. His *Kennedy's Children, Mr Cinders* and *Artist Descending A Staircase* end up on Broadway.

1970

Barbara Castle MP introduces Equal Pay Act.

1972

Rosie Boycott edits *Spare Rib*, Britain's first feminist newspaper from Clerkenwell Close. She draws attention to the strange convention of using scantily clad women to advertise anything from cars to carpets and to a predominance of sexist language. She is the first to challenge Advertising Standards Authority (ASA) which dismisses the idea that there is sexism in advertising. It takes her twenty years to educate the press against using politically incorrect language. The magazine covers topics such as Equal Pay for Equal Jobs, abortion law, women and the law, sexual equality, sexual harassment in the work place, health and the arts. Boycott at 21 is the youngest magazine editor in Britain. The first cover shows two women wearing no make up sharing a joke, in contrast to the covers of glamour magazines. Inside are feature articles on Erin Pizzey's Women's Refuge, a new abortion referral unit in Liverpool and NHS vasectomies. Fiction is by John Berger, Margaret Drabble, Eva Figes, Erica Jong, Edna O'Brien and Fay Weldon. Stickers 'This Advertisement Exploits Women' start appearing on London Underground.

1973

For the next decade, queues stretch two miles around the block to get into The Hope and Anchor to see The Damned, Dexy's Midnight Runners, Dire Straits, Ian Dury and The Blockheads (ex Kilburn & The High Roads) Eddie and the Hot Rods, Elvis Costello and The Attractions, Dr Feelgood, Frankie Goes To Hollywood, Generation X, Tim Hardin, Joe Jackson, The Jam, Joy Division, Long John Baldry, Madness, Q Tips, Tom Robinson Band, Shakin' Stevens, Squeeze, Sting, Steel Pulse, The Stranglers (who lived above the pub) Joe Strummer, The Vibrators, Wayne County and The Electric Chairs, X Ray Specs et al.

1975

Barbara Castle MP needs a political adviser on the NHS, husband Ted, Alderman for Islington Council, recommends the young Jack Straw, a barrister and effective Islington Councillor (vice Chair, Islington Council Housing Committee 1971 to 1978, deputy leader ILEA). His father was a conscientious objector his mother, in her 70s, an Islington councillor.

1976

(i) Poster: The Screen on the Green presents a Midnight Special Sunday Aug 29th Midnight-Dawn. On Stage Sex Pistols + Clash + Buzzcocks Tickets £1 from SEX 430 King's Road Chelsea's Tel 351 6764 pm. or Box Office Screen on The Green Tel 226 3520 This is a landmark gig for Lydon' I am the anti-chrrrrrrrrist!!!! I am an anarchisssst!!!!' (less of a group than an attitude).With them is a band so new it has no name. Suzie, lead singer, is wearing fishnet stockings, black cupless bra, swastika arm band and odd shoes. Siouxsie and the Banshees cause as much a stir as Johnny Rotten. Before Johnny Rotten (skinny, with staring menacing eyes, green hair, rotten teeth, ripped clothes held together with safety pins) pop singers, clean and pretty crooned love songs.

(ii) Among Dame Alice Owen School's last pupils is John Keeble, Tony Hadley, Gary and Martin Kemp from Essex Road and Steve Norman from Rosebery Avenue frothing to be pop stars. They form The Makers/The Cut/The Gentry. Three years later, the Godfathers of The New Romantics are Spandau Ballet. In 1999 they are fighting among themselves at the High Court in a multi million pound royalties wrangle.

1977

(i) Silver Jubilee. Local Sex Pistol John Lydon (Johnny Rotten) writes *God Save The Queen* (A fascist regime, She aint no human being, But god save the queen, There is no future to England's dream) on the kitchen table at home, a council flat in Finsbury Park waiting for his baked beans to heat up.

(ii) Bob Geldof (later formed The Boomtown Rats) joins old school mates in a filthy derelict squat in Tufnell Park Road reeking of dog pee, rotting carpets, leaking gas and of course marijuana. He amuses himself by setting up elaborate mouse traps and catches 26 in one night. One of the gang sees god on a LSD trip, joins a monastery and misses a drugs bust. In 1984 his *Do They Know its Christmas* for Band Aid sells 7m copies. He becomes Sir Bob in 1986.

1978

Signs of the times... Sisterwrite Bookshop, first feminist bookshop in the UK opens in Upper Street. The five woman co-operative (run by women for women about women) sells radical feminist literature from all over the world. The Women's Press with a flat iron logo, a new feminist publishing company, opens in an empty warehouse in Great Sutton Street Clerkenwell. At a Gay Rally in the Midlands Chris Smith MP (whose grandparents went to Dame Alice Owen School Islington): My name is Chris Smith I am the Labour MP for Islington South and I'm gay. His constituents vote him in for the next twenty years each time with an increased majority. After Dan Crawford and his King's Head Theatre Islington re-invents itself into off off Broadway, the empty Lit & Sci Building in Almeida Street is sold to founders of Almeida Theatre. Landlords of the Old Red Lion St John Street turn their sitting room into a theatre. Sixty punters take their bar stools with them to watch the show. 'Names' such as Susan Penhaligon, Daniel Day Lewis, Gary Oldman sponsor proper chairs at £75 each.

1979

The Islington branch of Hotblack Desiato, estate agent, find fame in Douglas Adams' *The Restaurant At The End of The Universe*.

1980

Islingtonian Lucy Irvine replies to an ad. in *Time Out* for 'a wife' to live on a desert island. She writes a best seller about her experiences which is turned into a film, *Castaway*, with Oliver Reed and Amanda Donoghue.

1981

Tariq Ali political activist opens The Other Book Shop at 328 Upper Street.

1982

Michael Fagan, painter and decorator, of Holloway Road, a single parent of six hops over the wall of Buckingham Palace and disturbs the Queen's beauty sleep. He says the palace could do with a face lift.

1986

(i) Cherie Booth returns to her roots when she moves into 10 Stavordale Road (her father, Anthony, said they are connected to the Clerkenwell Wilkes Booth's).

(ii) A stand up comedy venue opens in the Labour Party office, Seven Sisters Road. The Red Rose Comedy Club helps kick start David Baddiel, Jo Brand, Julian Clary, Alan Davies, Lee Evans, Hattie Hayridge, John Hegley, Eddie Izzard Paul Merton, Rob Newman, Gerry Sadowitz and Frank Skinner.

(iii) The old Aggie gets a new lease of life when Sam Morris re-opens it as The Business Design Centre (BDC).

(iv) George Orwell's old drinking haunt The Hen and Chickens, Highbury Corner, opens a theatre in its upstairs room.

(v) Esther Rantzen launches Childline in Theberton Street.

(vi) London Greenpeace Caledonian Road distributes leaflets *What's Wrong With McDonalds?* triggering a legal drama which lasts ten years.

1988

(i) African National Congress (ANC) Holloway is campaigning for Nelson Mandela's release from prison.

(ii) Charter 88 is set up.

(iii) Salman Rushdie is forced to sell his home in Islington and go into hiding, under sentence of death for publishing *The Satanic Verses*.

1990

Councillors leaving a meeting at Town Hall to implement Mrs Thatcher's Poll Tax are bombarded with missiles.

1991

(i) Population is 164,686.

(ii) The Crafts Council of Great Britain relocate to Pentonville from Lower Regent Street.

1992

(i) Mrs Bottomley, Minister for Health tries what Henry VIII tried. To close Barts. She also failed.

(ii) Nick Hornby puts his beloved Arsenal FC in *Fever Pitch*. In 1995 a second hand record shop in Holloway Road stars in *High Fidelity* and in 1999 he writes *About a Boy* a pupil a Highbury Grove School.

1993

(i) John Smith addresses Charter 88.

(ii) Holloway Road, the first red route in London with the first spy speed trap cameras (no stopping from the Archway to the Angel).

1994

(i) John Smith Leader of the Labour Party, dies. Mr Blair of Barnsbury meets Gordon Brown at the Granita restaurant Upper Street and asks permission to be the new leader.

(ii) Paul Jackson, Islington Councillor, expert on microwave technology helps in the grisly hunt for Fred and Rosemary West's victims.

1995

Charter 88 holds a public debate on the future of the monarchy.

1996

(i) Pilgrims visit Chapel Market to consult with 'Fergie's' medium, 'Madame Vasso' in her famous purple pyramid.

(ii) Archway Clinic of Herbal Medicine the first within a NHS hospital (Whittington) treats patients with artichokes, celery and dandelions.

(iii) A plaque to Joe (*Telstar*) Meek is put on his recording studio by local Islington tourist guides Pamela Shields and David Andrews with funds raised by John Repsch, his biographer, Secretary of the Joe Meek Appreciation Society.

1997

(i) Art '97. British Design Centre. Silver coated plaster cast Head and Torso. £4500. The sculptor is found guilty of stealing body parts and spends six weeks in Brixton nick.

(ii) Diana, Princess of Wales dies. David Hillman, Campaigns officer for the UK Working Group on Landmines, Holloway Road said she put landmines in everybody's living room.

1999

(i) Population 180,000. Andrew Motion of Tufnell Park is appointed poet laureate.

(ii) The Angel, Islington gets a statue for the Millennium.

(iii) BAFTA ceremony held in the old Aggie. Supposedly up and coming since the Clean Air Act of 1956, has Islington finally arrived?

2020

Forecast: Ian Crawley, Islington Council Town Planner. Population 210,000; few families; young people with high salaries living in Islington's 3000 lofts communicating via Internet; car clubs hiring a vehicle when they need one; 24 trains an hour at King's Cross Channel Tunnel Rail Link makes the area a Mecca for travellers, home buyers and shoppers; The hated Archway Tower has gone; the glass roof (bombed WWII) is back on St Pancras; increase in Vegetarians following the BSE crisis; Smithfield Market closed, the area rivals Covent Garden; St John Street is an extension of Upper Street looking much as it did in the days of the drovers with pubs and eating places tumbling over one another

Printed in Great Britain
by Amazon